BILLY GRAHAM
Evangelistic Association

DEAR FRIEND,

What do the Ten Commandments mean to us today? Why should we obey them?

The following 11 Bible studies were published in *Decision* magazine beginning in January 2000. The response was dramatic—requests came by letter, telephone, and e-mail for copies of the complete series. As a result, we decided to publish the series in this book format.

Our system of justice is based largely upon these Commandments, and they are accepted as a foundation for the Judeo-Christian faith. Yet few people today can name more than a few of the Commandments. In this book, prominent Christian teachers discuss the Commandments and how they are relevant to our lives today.

Read the articles in each section, then answer the study questions that follow. The questions offer an opportunity for you to dig deeper into God's Word. You may wish to use them, as so many others have, in your personal study, a family Bible study, a Sunday school class or in other group settings.

I pray that these studies will help you delight more and more in God's law. Then you will be like the blessed man in Psalm 1, who *"is like a tree planted by streams of water, which yields its fruit in season and whose leaf does not wither. Whatever he does prospers"* (v. 3, NIV).

May God richly bless you.

Sincerely,

Franklin Graham
President and CEO

FOUNDATIONS *for* LIFE

REFLECTIONS ON JOYFUL OBEDIENCE
FROM THE TEN COMMANDMENTS

BILLY
GRAHAM
Evangelistic Association

This **Billy Graham Library Selection** special edition
is published by the Billy Graham Evangelistic Association.

Chapters I through XI originally published as a series during 2000 in *Decision* magazine, ©1999, 2000 Billy Graham Evangelistic Association, 1 Billy Graham Parkway, Charlotte, NC 28201, U.S.A.

Scripture quotations marked NKJV are taken from the *New King James Version.* ©1982 Thomas Nelson, Inc., Publishers. Used by permission. All rights reserved.

Scripture quotations marked NIV are taken from *The Holy Bible: New International Version.* ©1973, 1978, 1984 by International Bible Society. Used by permission. All rights reserved.

Scripture quotations marked NASB are taken from the *New American Standard Bible.* ©1960, 1962, 1963, 1968, 1971, 1972, 1973, 1975, 1977 The Lockman Foundation. Used by permission.

Scripture quotations marked RSV are taken from *The Holy Bible: Revised Standard Version.* ©1946, 1952 by Division of Christian Education of the National Council of the Churches of Christ in the United States of America. Used by permission.

Scripture quotations marked NLT are taken from the Holy Bible, *New Living Translation.* ©1996 Tyndale Charitable Trust. Used by permission. All rights reserved.

Scripture quotations marked KJV are taken from the King James Version.

ISBN: 978-1-59328-040-6
Previous ISBN: 0-913367-33-8

Printed in the United States of America

THE TEN COMMANDMENTS

AND GOD SPOKE ALL THESE WORDS, SAYING: I am the Lord your God, who brought you out of the land of Egypt, out of the house of bondage.

1 *YOU SHALL HAVE NO OTHER GODS BEFORE ME.*

2 *YOU SHALL NOT MAKE FOR YOURSELF A CARVED IMAGE—any likeness of anything that is in heaven above, or that is in the earth beneath, or that is in the water under the earth; you shall not bow down to them nor serve them. For I, the Lord your God, am a jealous God, visiting the iniquity of the fathers upon the children to the third and fourth generations of those who hate Me, but showing mercy to thousands, to those who love Me and keep My commandments.*

3 *YOU SHALL NOT TAKE THE NAME OF THE LORD YOUR GOD IN VAIN, for the Lord will not hold him guiltless who takes His name in vain.*

4 *REMEMBER THE SABBATH DAY, to keep it holy. Six days you shall labor and do all your work, but the seventh day is the Sabbath of the Lord your God. In it you shall do no work: you, nor your son, nor your daughter, nor your male servant, nor your female servant, nor your cattle, nor your stranger who is within your gates. For in six days the Lord made the heavens and the earth, the sea, and all that is in them, and rested the seventh day. Therefore the Lord blessed the Sabbath day and hallowed it.*

5 *HONOR YOUR FATHER AND YOUR MOTHER, that your days may be long upon the land which the Lord your God is giving you.*

6 *YOU SHALL NOT MURDER.*

7 *YOU SHALL NOT COMMIT ADULTERY.*

8 *YOU SHALL NOT STEAL.*

9 *YOU SHALL NOT BEAR FALSE WITNESS against your neighbor.*

10 *YOU SHALL NOT COVET your neighbor's house; you shall not covet your neighbor's wife, nor his male servant, nor his female servant, nor his ox, nor his donkey, nor anything that is your neighbor's.*

—Exodus 20:1–17, NKJV

Contents

THE FIRST COMMANDMENT: EXODUS 20:2–3

YOU SHALL HAVE NO OTHER GODS BEFORE ME.

IS GOD FIRST IN OUR HEARTS?

:: *BY JOHN N. AKERS*

He was a star athlete at the college where I was teaching—popular, personable and a good student as well. Now he sat across from me in shock, staggered by the news he had just received: He was being suspended for cheating.

"I didn't think anyone took those rules seriously," he complained, shaking his head in stunned disbelief. "After all, what's right for someone else isn't necessarily right for me. Rules are made to be broken!"

My heart went out to him, not just because of the disgrace he had brought upon himself, but because he had fallen for one of the devil's oldest (and most popular) lies: There is no such thing as right and wrong. But God has taught us otherwise—and that makes all the difference. Some actions are always right or always wrong, and refusing to live by God's moral standards only brings us heartache and disaster.

The Ten Commandments summarize God's moral standards for His people, and that is why they are still valid. (You can find them in Exodus 20:1–17 and Deuteronomy 5:7–21.) And they are just as important today as they were when God gave them through Moses to the ancient Israelites more than 3,000 years ago.

Heading the list is the First Commandment: *"You shall have no other gods before me."*[1] Not only is it first in location but first in importance, for from it all the other Commandments flow, and without it they lose their authority.

THE ONE WHO SPEAKS

We will take this (or any other) Commandment seriously

only when we understand who gave it: *"And God spoke all these words."*[2] The Ten Commandments were not the product of a royal decree or a popular poll; they came from God Himself.

Think what this means. It means, first, that behind the Ten Commandments is the full, absolute authority of God Himself. The God of the universe has spoken! What right, therefore, do we have to ignore His words or twist their meaning? Who are we to think that our ways are better than His? The only logical response to God's Commandments must be obedience, for "he who gives men their lives has most right to give them their laws."[3] You may have heard the old saying: "Wherever God has placed a period, don't try to change it to a question mark!"

It means also that we should prayerfully listen to these Commandments, asking God to open our hearts and minds and to help us understand the meaning of His Commandments. Like young Samuel, our prayer to God should be, *"Speak, for your servant is listening."*[4] Is this your prayer whenever you open God's Word?

But we also will only take the Ten Commandments seriously when we understand what God had already done for His people: *"I am the Lord your God, who brought you out of Egypt, out of the land of slavery."*[5]

For 430 years—10 generations—the Israelites had languished in slavery,[6] oppressed by their harsh Egyptian taskmasters and driven to the brink of despair. Now God had heard their prayers and freed them from their slavery, even destroying Pharaoh's army in the process. God in His grace and love had reached out and saved them.

In the same way, the New Testament teaches that apart from Christ we too are slaves—slaves of sin, living under the domination of a cruel taskmaster named Satan. But God has provided the way out of our slavery, through the shed blood of Jesus Christ. Before coming to Christ, *"we were in slavery under the basic principles of the world. But when the time had fully come, God sent his Son. ... So you are no longer a slave, but a son."*[7] Have you trusted Christ as your Savior and Lord? If so, you are now part of His family forever, set free from the penalty and the power of sin.

WHY HE GAVE HIS COMMANDMENTS

With freedom, however, comes responsibility. God did not deliver the Israelites from slavery so that they could live any way they pleased. He had a plan for them that could be fulfilled only if they followed His will. Furthermore, God knew that unrestrained freedom eventually results in its own kind of slavery—a slavery to selfishness and lust. God loved His people too much to allow them to drift through life without His guidance. Just as a parent knows what is best for a child, so God knew what was best for the Israelites.

Therefore He gave them the Commandments, so that they would know how best to live: *"Hear, O Israel, and be careful to obey so that it may go well with you."*[8] If they refused to follow His path, they would never enjoy the blessings of His love, nor would they fulfill His plan for their lives.

So it is with us. When we know Christ, we know that God loves us and has a perfect plan for our lives. We know also that we are not free to live any way we want to. Instead, we each have a responsibility *"to put off [our] old self, which is being corrupted by its deceitful desires, ... and to put on the new self, created to be like God in true righteousness and holiness."*[9]

Why obey the Ten Commandments as well as all of God's will? Not to win our salvation—for Christ in His love and grace has already purchased it for us through His death on the cross. Our works can never save us; Christ alone is our hope.

Instead, we obey the Commandments because we are now God's children, and we want to please our loving heavenly Father out of gratitude for all that He has done for us. Jesus said, *"If you love me, you will obey what I command."*[10] We obey Him also because God's way is always best for us, for God's will comes from His love.

THE COMMAND HE GAVE

The First Commandment is deceptively simple, only eight words in our English text: *"You shall have no other gods before me."*[1]

All their lives these Israelites had been surrounded by the idolatry and polytheism of Egypt. Every pyramid, every monument, every public ceremony, proclaimed a deep-seated belief in many gods and goddesses. Furthermore, the Israelites would be facing the same kind of situation in the future, both during their wilderness wanderings and in Canaan. The pressure to give in to the pagan beliefs of those around them would be intense.

Nothing was more critical, therefore, than underlining the urgency of holding fast to God alone, which is what these words command. Professor Ronald S. Wallace has summarized it this way: "Here, then, in the First Commandment, we are faced with an issue of life or death for the people of God. It is a warning against falling back into an outlook, a bondage of heart and mind, from which they have been once-for-all delivered by what God has done for them in His love." [11]

What does it mean to *"have no other gods before me"* [1]? The Hebrew phrase "before me" is an unusual one. It can speak of faithfulness in marriage, with both husband and wife allowing no rivals to take the rightful place of their spouse. It also can be translated "against" [12] me or "in defiance of me." [12] The meaning is clear: God only must have first place in our lives. Nothing must come between Him and us.

PUTTING GOD FIRST

We may not think that polytheism (a belief in many gods) is our problem today. Or is it? A "god," after all, is anything (or anyone) that we allow to have first place in our life. A "god" is anything which dominates or controls us, becoming the focus of our attention and the object of our affection.

Think of the "gods" that preoccupy our world today. For some people it may be the "god" of pleasure, or beauty, or entertainment, or money, or sex, or possessions, or social position, or a relationship, or power. Other people find their "god" in false spiritualities, or religions, or occult practices. Still other people allow some emotion to overpower and control them instead of God: anger, jealousy, pride, bitterness, an unforgiving spirit. Even Christians may allow themselves to be blinded by the spirit of our age, falling into the trap of materialism or self-love or some specific sin.

But the Bible is clear: There is only one true God: *"I am God, and there is no other; I am God, and there is none like me."*[13] All other "gods" are false.

How do we live out this Commandment? First, we must examine ourselves, prayerfully and carefully, and then repent of anything—any sin, any false god—which we have allowed to take God's rightful place. Is God and His will first in our hearts? I recall the saying I first heard as a teenager: "If Christ is not Lord of all, then He is not Lord at all."

Second, we must commit ourselves without reserve to God and His Word. We must actively put Him first, daily seeking His face and doing His will in the power of the Holy Spirit. We must truly *"have no other gods before [him]."*[1] When God rules our lives, we will never be the same.

---

(1) Exodus 20:3, NIV. (2) Exodus 20:1, NIV. (3) From *The Ten Commandments*, by Thomas Watson, published by The Banner of Truth Trust, London, England, 1959. (4) 1 Samuel 3:10, NIV. (5) Exodus 20:2, NIV. (6) Exodus 12:40. (7) Galatians 4:3–4, 7, NIV. (8) Deuteronomy 6:3, NIV. (9) Ephesians 4:22, 24, NIV. (10) John 14:15, NIV. (11) From *The Ten Commandments: A Study of Ethical Freedom*, by Ronald S. Wallace, ©1965 R.S. Wallace, Wm. B. Eerdmans Publishing Company, Grand Rapids, Michigan. (12) From "The Ten Commandments in Recent Research," by J.J. Stamm and M.E. Andrew, in *Studies in Biblical Theology*, Second Series (translated from *Der DeKalog im Lichte der neueren Forschung*, 1962), ©1967 SCM Press Ltd., London, England. (13) Isaiah 46:9, NIV.

John N. Akers, Ph.D., is special assistant to Billy Graham and works for the Billy Graham Evangelistic Association, in Montreat, North Carolina. He and his wife, Anne, are parents of one son. ©1999 Billy Graham Evangelistic Association.

DO WE WORSHIP GOD— OR GODS?

:: BY G. CAMPBELL MORGAN

It has been said that when man dethrones God, he deifies and worships himself. There are people today of whom it may be said that they worship themselves with all their heart and with all their strength and with all their mind, and themselves only do they serve.

The moment a person gets out of touch with God and loses the vision of Him who says, "I am Jehovah Elohim, the Lord thy God,"[1] he puts something else in the place of God.

Think of the gods of the heathen as mentioned in the Bible— Molech, Baal and Mammon. The worship of Molech was the descent of man into the realm of awful cruelty; that of Baal took men through the depths of bestiality and impurity; and that of Mammon debased its devotees to the lust which dreams that power lurks in possession.

Molech, Baal and Mammon were the gods of the heathen, and people are worshiping them to this hour. Although these gods go by other names in this cultured and enlightened age, the world is crowded with idolaters who worship them.

People deal with God only as a last resource, and yet they go on hoping to sneak into God's heaven when they are done with His world. But the God of Sinai is thundering out to this age, "Thou shalt put Me first, and the business second."[2]

If people put Molech, Baal, Mammon, or appetites or anything else into the place that demands devotion and energy to God, they are idolaters. People were made for the God who declares that His creatures shall have no other god before Him.

Let people take five minutes to shut out everything except the fact that they stand alone with God. Let them ask, as they stand in the light of that First Commandment, "What is my god? To what is my life devoted?" If the answer indicates anything that puts God into the background, then let them "break down every idol, cast out every foe,"[3] and let the God who will be, who is, who was, be their God.

---

(1) Cf. Deuteronomy 5:9. (2) Cf. Exodus 20:3. (3) From "Whiter Than Snow," by James L. Nicholson.

G. Campbell Morgan (1863–1945) was a British Congregational minister. A lecturer and a Bible teacher, he traveled widely in the United States and in Canada in evangelistic and preaching missions. He was the author of 60 books and a dozen booklets. This message was taken from *The Ten Commandments*, by G. Campbell Morgan, ©1901 The Bible Institute Colportage Association of Chicago, Fleming H. Revell Company, a division of Baker Book House Company, Grand Rapids, Michigan; used by permission of the Reverend G. Campbell Morgan Estate, London, England.

FOUNDATIONS FOR LIFE
:: A CLOSER LOOK ::

The First Commandment: *"I am the Lord your God. ... You shall have no other gods before Me"* (Exodus 20:2–3, NKJV).

OBSERVE

1. Take a few minutes to read through the Ten Commandments (Exodus 20:1–17). In addition to our relationship with God, what other relationships are addressed in the Commandments? _____

   _____

   _____

2. Look at Exodus 19:1, 16; Deuteronomy 9:9–12; and Exodus 32:1. From the time that God led the Israelites out of Egypt, how long did it take for the people to fall back into idolatry?

   _____

   _____

   _____

INTERPRET

1. Why do you think that God prefaced His Commandments the way that He did?

   Exodus 20:2 _____

   _____

   _____

2. How does Jesus' summary of the Law enhance our understanding of the First Commandment?

   Matthew 22:34–40 _____

   _____

3. List some of the "gods" that people serve today, and read Jesus' warning about serving two masters. Why would serving another god cause us to "hate" or "despise" God?

Matthew 6:24 _____

_____

_____

Apply

1. In Deuteronomy 5 Moses repeated the story of how God gave the Ten Commandments. In verse 1, what three things did He urge the people to do? Pray that these will be true in your study of God's Word.

Deuteronomy 5:1 _____

_____

_____

2. Read David's prayer in Psalm 139:23–24. Are you allowing any other gods to usurp God's rightful place in your life? Ask God to search your heart, then yield yourself afresh to Him and to His will. _____

_____

_____

_____

_____

ARE WE IDOLATERS?

:: *BY WALTER C. KAISER JR.*

As my wife, Marge, and I were being driven from Baguio City to the airport in Manila, the Philippines, some years ago, we were both struck by the innumerable god-houses that lined the roadway in front of almost every house. In contrast to the poor and often wretched condition of their own homes, the god-houses seemed to have all the wealth and workmanship that the people themselves seemed to lack. Similar scenes greeted us in Japan. There the huge temples were elaborate structures.

In Athens, Corinth and other major cities that the Apostle Paul visited, one is also struck by the elaborate attention that generations past have poured out on their idols and nonexistent gods.

In so many parts of the world we have seen the ironic picture that the Prophet Isaiah described.[1] Craftsmen cut down trees in order to fashion a god. Approximately one-half of the tree ends up being used for fuel to warm the craftsman and his family or to bake bread and roast meat. But from the other half the worker makes an idol in the form of what he conceives to be his god. To this creation he now bows down and worships!

But doesn't anyone stop to think about what he or she is doing? Can these hunks of wood see? Can they think? How can this idol save the worshiper? The minds of such worshipers feed on ashes and their hearts mislead them, charges Isaiah.[2] What is more, men and women tend to become like that which they worship!

God warns precisely against such worship: "*You shall not make for yourself an idol in the form of anything in heaven above or on the earth beneath or in the waters below. You shall not bow down to them or worship them; for I, the Lord your God, am a jealous God, punishing the children for the sin of the*

fathers to the third and fourth generation of those who hate me,
but showing love to a thousand generations of those who love me
and keep my commandments."[3]

This Second Commandment may be examined under its
three parts. First, there is the precept itself, which has two
prohibitions: (a) forbidding images to be made,[4] (b)
forbidding them to be worshiped.[5] Second, there is a severe
rebuke against those who presume to violate this
Commandment.[5] Third, the Commandment ends with an
encouragement for obedience to this command.[6] Let us look at
each of these three parts of this Commandment.

OUR CALL TO WORSHIP PROPERLY

Some have incorrectly argued that this command is directed
against all creativity and artistry of the carver, the painter and
the sculptor. But instead of the command being a freeze on
artistic skill, it is a blow at worshiping what we have created
rather than worshiping the Creator Himself.

Consider that God commanded that a *"bronze snake"*[7] be
made in the wilderness, that cherubim be fashioned for the
tabernacle[8] and that numerous artistic motifs be included in
the Tabernacle and in the Temple. That is enough to call for a
reconsideration of any antiartistic or iconoclastic interpretation
of this Commandment.

The precept in Exodus 20:4–6 does not declare that it is
unlawful to make a representation of what the eye sees. The two
"You shall nots"[9] are to be viewed together in this manner: You
shall not make anything with an intention of worshiping it. Just
as the First Commandment dealt with the spiritual and internal
attitudes and affections of a person, so the Second
Commandment deals with the more external and visible
adoration of anything except God. The problem is with giving
reverential adoration to the images that one makes instead of
worshiping God alone.

The worship of God, in external forms, is just as spiritual as
the internal attitudes decreed in the First Commandment, for it
too proceeds from the Spirit of God. The worship moves our

wills in acts of celebration of the ordinances of the Church, in solemn prayer and in exuberant praise and thanksgiving to our heavenly Father. Since God has made both the body and the soul, and sustains both, He expects homage and service from both. Therefore the body must enter into the worship of God along with our spirits.

At its heart, idolatry is superstition. Idolatry gives divine honors to that which is not God. The Apostle Paul was grieved when he saw the idolatry of Athens,[10] and when he reproved them, he chided them for their superstition.[11] Accordingly, even though not all superstition is idolatry, all idolatry is superstition.

Who in modern society is an idolater? He or she is an idolater who prays to some creature or something—for in so doing he or she ascribes to that creature or object the honor that belongs solely to the Creator.

Another form of idolatry, perhaps most commonly seen in the West, is placing any person, idea, goal or thing in a position that is equal to, or greater than, God. God will not share His glory or honor with any other person or thing. God deserves first place: no rivals, period.

OUR PROMISED MERCY FOR OBEDIENCE

The One who graciously promised to show mercy to those who love Him and who keep His Commandments says of Himself, *"I, the Lord your God, am a jealous God."*[12] He is our God (if we have trusted in Him for our salvation) because we have been betrothed to him.[13] That is why idolatry is the same as spiritual harlotry. It marries us off to a spouse other than the sovereign Lord to whom we are betrothed.

All rivalries to God's unique place provoke His jealousy. Jealousy, when used of God, is not a passion that wants to get even or to get revenge; it is an affection or passion of the mind stirring itself and being provoked by all that hinders the enjoyment of that which we love and desire. This concept is caused by God's love.

The expression "jealousy" is used by way of accommodation to us mortals—not that God has the same inner affections but only the same outward effects. And of all sins, there is none that God observes more closely and jealously than that of idolatry. It is a violation of our marriage-faith to Him. Therefore we must ask, *"Are we trying to arouse the Lord's jealousy? Are we stronger than he?"*[14] It is a fearful thing to fall into the hands of the living God, for *"the Lord your God is a consuming fire, a jealous God."*[15]

What will God do to idolaters who break covenant with Him? In the King James Version the text reads: *"I the Lord thy God am a jealous God, visiting the iniquity of the fathers upon the children."*[16] Such "visiting" is a figurative expression, but in its negative sense it means that God will reward such sins with their deserved and just punishments.

But is such punishment fair and just? Did not the Prophet Ezekiel teach that *"the soul who sins is the one who will die"*[17]? The answer is this: If children imitate the offenses of their fathers, they too will die in their sins. God is justified in punishing, but God never "visits" the iniquity of the fathers upon repenting children, giving them eternal punishments.

Indeed, there may be temporal punishments in this life that come as a result of the offenses of the fathers. Here again, however, God does not always bring temporal punishments upon the children of erring parents. King Hezekiah, the son of rebellious King Ahaz, and King Josiah, the son of wicked King Amon, were righteous and prosperous, despite their parents' horrid record with God.[18] How much greater is the effect of God's mercy and love for those who love Him: It extends to thousands of generations!

OUR ENCOURAGEMENT TO OBEDIENCE

Most parents try to leave to their children estates that are not clogged up with legal obstructions or with unpaid debts. But have some parents been negligent about leaving their children a host of plagues and curses for their posterity?

In the end idolatry is not only the worship of crafted forms and shapes ascribed to some deity. It is also putting anyone or anything, even goals, in our lives equal with, or superior to, the living God. When we put our jobs, our careers, our children, our churches, our institutions, our spouses or our education equal to, or ahead of, God, we are headlong into idolatry!

Those who were born into families who worshiped only the one true God need to thank Him for godly parents who trusted the Savior and who loved God. That heritage is not a small gift.

But how do we define those who love God? The Apostle John described such a person: *"Whoever has my commands and obeys them, he is the one who loves me."* [19] But those who transgress the Commandments are those who hate God and goodness.

Finally, note the mercy of God even in the threatened duration of the punishment: The duration is only to the third and fourth generation. [5] The mercy is that the race of people was not cut off and thrown out of God's sight and grace forever. As always, God's grace and mercy exceed His judgment. Thanks be to God!

---

(1) Isaiah 44:13–20. (2) Isaiah 44:20. (3) Exodus 20:4–6, NIV. (4) Exodus 20:4. (5) Exodus 20:5. (6) Exodus 20:6. (7) Numbers 21:9, NIV. (8) Exodus 25:18; 37:7. (9) Exodus 20:4–5, NIV. (10) Acts 17:16. (11) Acts 17:22. (12) Exodus 20:5, NIV. (13) Isaiah 54:5. (14) 1 Corinthians 10:22, NIV. (15) Deuteronomy 4:24, NIV. (16) Exodus 20:5, KJV. (17) Ezekiel 18:20, NIV. (18) 2 Kings 18:1–6. (19) John 14:21, NIV.

Walter C. Kaiser Jr., Ph.D., is distinguished professor of Old Testament and president of Gordon-Conwell Theological Seminary, in South Hamilton, Massachusetts. He is the author of hundreds of articles and more than 30 books, including *The Christian and the Old Testament* and *Revive Us Again*. He and his wife, Marge, are parents of four grown children and live in South Hamilton. ©2000 Billy Graham Evangelistic Association.

GOD'S INTENSE JEALOUSY

:: *BY WAYNE A. GRUDEM*

The creation language in this Commandment (*"heaven above, or ... earth beneath, or ... water under the earth"*[1]) is a reminder that God's *being*, His essential mode of existence, is different from everything that He has created. To think of His being in terms of anything else in the created universe is to misrepresent Him, to limit Him, to think of Him as less than He really is.

To make a *"graven [or carved or sculptured] image"*[1] of God, as a golden calf for example, may have been an attempt to portray God as a God who is strong and full of life (like a calf), but to say that God was like a calf was a terribly false statement about God's knowledge, wisdom, love, mercy, omnipresence, eternity, independence, holiness, righteousness, justice, and so forth.

Indeed, while we must say that God has made all creation so that each part of it reflects something of His own character, we must also affirm that to picture God as *existing* in a form or mode of *being* that is like anything else in creation is to think of God in a way that is horribly misleading and dishonoring.

God is jealous to protect His own honor: *"For I the Lord your God am a jealous God."*[2] He eagerly seeks for people to think of Him as He is and to worship Him for all His excellence, and He is angered when His glory is diminished or His character is falsely represented.[3] God's intense jealousy for His own honor is given as the reason for a prohibition against making any images of Him.

---

(1) Exodus 20:4, RSV. (2) Exodus 20:5, RSV. (3) Deuteronomy 4:23–24.

Wayne A. Grudem, Ph.D., is research professor of Bible and theology at Phoenix Seminary, in Phoenix, Arizona. He is the author of numerous books and articles. He and his wife, Margaret, are parents of three grown children. This article is taken by permission from *Systematic Theology: An Introduction to Biblical Doctrine,* by Wayne A. Grudem, ©1994 Wayne Grudem, Inter-Varsity Press, Leicester, England, and Zondervan Publishing House, a division of HarperCollins Publishers, Grand Rapids, Michigan.

FOUNDATIONS FOR LIFE
:: A CLOSER LOOK ::

The Second Commandment: *"You shall not make for yourself a carved image—any likeness of anything that is in heaven above, or that is in the earth beneath, or that is in the water under the earth; you shall not bow down to them nor serve them. For I, the Lord your God, am a jealous God, visiting the iniquity of the fathers upon the children to the third and fourth generations of those who hate Me, but showing mercy to thousands, to those who love Me and keep My commandments"* (Exodus 20:4–6, NKJV).

OBSERVE

1. What are the two specific prohibitions regarding idols mentioned in Exodus 20:4–5? _____

_____

_____

2. What does God promise for those who don't keep His Commandments? What does He promise those who obey His Commandments?

Exodus 20:5 _____

_____

Exodus 20:6 _____

_____

3. How does the Prophet Isaiah portray the folly of idolatry?

Isaiah 44:13–20 _____

_____

_____

INTERPRET

1. According to the Apostle Paul, what are some sinful characteristics that constitute idolatry?

Ephesians 5:5 _____

_____

2. What does it mean that God is *a jealous God*?

Exodus 20:5 _____

_____

Deuteronomy 4:23–24_____

_____

2 Corinthians 11:2 _____

_____

3. Can we be satisfied with worshiping God internally, only in our hearts, or should our worship also take an external form?

Luke 19:36–40 _____

_____

APPLY

1. List some external forms of worship of God. Commit to making worship part of your daily walk with Christ.

_____

_____

2. Do you have things in your life that you have allowed to usurp from God the honor, respect and glory that belongs only to Him? Submit yourself to God, and pray that He will take His rightful place in your life.

_____

_____

THE THIRD COMMANDMENT: EXODUS 20:7

You shall not take the name of the Lord your God in vain.

WHAT DOES IT REALLY MEAN TO TAKE THE LORD'S NAME IN VAIN?

:: *BY LAWSON G. STONE*

In the *Journal of the American Medical Association*[1] Dr. Howard J. Bennett presented his personal study of the various names of people in the medical profession in the United States. In his study he found 22 doctors named Needle, Probe, Lance and Ligate, and another 20 named Drill, Scope, Bolt and Pin. Dr. Bennett also found 19 physicians named Fix, Cure and Heal, and 74 doctors named Brilliant, Able and Best! But imagine the ambivalence of a patient who visits doctors with names like Klutz or Croak! Today we may be amused when a person's name actually "fits" his character or profession. In Bible times, however, a person's name typically reflected something of his character or personality. Naturally, then, God cares deeply about His own name. Thus, in the Third Commandment, we read, *"You shall not take the name of the Lord your God in vain."*[2]

Whenever this Commandment comes to mind, we think first of the much-heard use of "God" in profanity. Those of us who are scrupulous about such uses of the word "God" or "Jesus" generally think that we've kept this Commandment. While it is good and proper to show a reverence for these words in our speech, a close inspection of the Commandment in the original language (Hebrew) and in the life of ancient Israel takes us far beyond the simple avoidance of sacrilegious speech.

MORE THAN DEITY

First, we are not to take the name of the "Lord our God"[3] in vain. The term "LORD," in all capital letters in the Old

Testament, is the personal name usually rendered as "Yahweh." This name was not a generic term for deity, but the personal name of the specific God who had a covenant relationship with His people, Israel. The phrase *"your God"*[2] also clearly tells us that the Commandment is aimed at people who have a relationship with this God. Therefore, the Commandment does not prohibit disrespectful speech about deity in general but addresses people who know a specific deity by a personal name.

Ancient Israel lived among cultures that worshiped scores of gods under a dizzying array of names and titles. The Old Testament contains many scathing verbal attacks on these other gods. Isaiah 40–55 bristles with repeated attacks on the gods of the Gentile nations. The Prophet Ezekiel, in referring to "idols," used 38 times a slang word meaning "dung pellets."[4] No basis existed during the lifetime of Moses for commanding that deity in general be respected.

Indeed, acceptance of the true God means absolute opposition to any other gods, as stated in the First Commandment.[5]

MORE THAN A WORD

In the Bible the idea of "name" carries much more weight than in our culture. A person's name was not simply a moniker; it also denoted a person's character and reputation. In Proverbs 22:1 we read, "A good name is better than great riches."[6] That proverb is referring to our reputations.

Repeatedly in the Old Testament the people appeal to God to act on behalf of His name. Obviously the people appealed to God to uphold His reputation, a reputation established by His mighty deeds of deliverance, guidance, judgment and provision—and also by His victory in granting Israel the Promised Land, thereby keeping the promises He had made to Israel's ancestors. When Moses came to Pharaoh saying, *"Thus says [Yahweh], Let my people go,"*[7] Pharaoh answered, "Who is Yahweh, that I should listen to him? I do not know Yahweh, and I will not let you go!"[8] In the plagues that followed, the recurring theme is that "they might know that I am Yahweh."[9] The plagues served as a historical, real-life dramatization of who this God Yahweh actually is.

Of course, the Bible warns against unclean speech of any kind.[10] But this Commandment emphasizes that those who name Yahweh, the God of Israel, as God, are entrusted with a responsibility for upholding God's reputation in the world. All that He has done for us, from the creation of the world through the miracles to the atoning death and the resurrection of Jesus Christ, is distilled into His name. In addition, the New Testament regularly treats the name of Jesus as a divine name, adding to the Third Commandment the concept of stewardship of the name and reputation of Jesus Christ. To take the name of the Lord in vain, then, is to take in vain the entire history of God's saving grace and to discredit the Gospel of Jesus Christ.

MORE THAN PROFANITY

But what does it really mean to take the name of the Lord "in vain"? The Hebrew term traditionally translated "in vain" has two basic, closely connected meanings. First, the term means "ineffectual, useless, empty."[11] God laments, in Jeremiah 2:30, that *"in vain I have struck your sons,"*[12] meaning that His chastisement has borne no fruit. Likewise, in Psalm 127:1–2, this very word, "vain," is used three times to emphasize the uselessness of ordinary human activity apart from the blessing of God. From this sense of uselessness comes a second meaning of the Hebrew term "in vain": "ultimately false and disappointing."[11] Clearly that which cannot work effectively will ultimately be proven false.

Substituting the sense of ineffectiveness, fruitlessness, uselessness and deceitfulness for the traditional "in vain" of the Commandment produces a shocking result. The declaration in the Third Commandment that we are not to take the reputation and saving work of our covenant-keeping God "in vain" points far beyond saying a form of God's name in an angry tone.

What it tells us is not to let God's name, and all that it implies, be ineffectual and meaningless in our lives. No doubt, this does relate to our speech! But more important, what is at stake in the Third Commandment is our stewardship of God's truth as He has revealed it. For the name of God to be ineffectual means that it has become merely a story in the past, a tradition devoid of dynamic power and life-changing impact.

This clearly happened in Israel's history: *"There arose another generation after them who did not know the Lord, nor yet the work which He had done for Israel."*[13] The verses that follow narrate Israel's catastrophic slide into apostasy and idolatry, leading to bondage and suffering under divine wrath.

What triggered the Israelites' worship of other gods, violating the First Commandment? What led to the Israelites' falling into idolatry, violating the Second Commandment? They *"did not know the Lord, nor yet the work which He had done for Israel."*[13] The Prophet Malachi accused his contemporaries repeatedly of profaning the name of God. God's name and deeds meant nothing to them. Perhaps the writer to the Hebrews had this in mind when, speaking to believers, he wrote, *"How shall we escape if we neglect so great a salvation?"*[14]

How many professing Christians, who are stewards of the name and image of Jesus Christ, have allowed His name, His character and His work in history and in their lives to count for nothing and to appear false to the world?

More Than Speech

It begins to sound as if the Third Commandment is not mainly about our talk—it's about our walk. That emerges clearly in this observation about the Commandment: *"You shall not take the name of the Lord your God in vain."*[2] The key to the entire Commandment lies in the word "take." What a shock it was to learn in my first-year Hebrew class that the word does not refer to speech! The Hebrew word means to "carry, bear." It can refer to speech in formal ways, such as when we "bear" good or bad tidings. Usually, though, it simply means to "carry." We are not to "carry" the name of the Lord our God ineffectually so that it appears false.

The Bible repeatedly summarizes our relationship with God under the phrase, "I shall be your God, and you shall be My people."[9] Hebrews 11:16 celebrates that God is not ashamed to be called our God. But what a risk God takes in entrusting His name and His reputation in the world to our fragile and failing hands!

We are charged then with not disappointing His trust in us. We must not be like those whom Jesus cast out in judgment, those who said, *"Lord, Lord, did we not prophesy in Your name, and in Your name cast out demons, and in Your name perform many miracles?"* [15] Because their lives did not show forth the reality and the truth of God's name, Jesus declared, *"I never knew you; depart from Me, you who practice lawlessness."* [16]

We are bearers of a great name. We cannot let that name seem powerless, ineffectual and false in our lives.

---

(1) See "Calling Dr. Doctor," by Howard J. Bennett, in *Journal of the American Medical Association*, December 2, 1992. (2) Exodus 20:7, NKJV. (3) Cf. Exodus 20:7. (4) In *Vine's Expository Dictionary of Biblical Words*, by W.E. Vine, Merrill F. Unger and William White Jr., ©1985 Thomas Nelson, Inc., Publishers, Nashville, Tennessee. (5) Exodus 20:3. (6) Cf. Proverbs 22:1. (7) Exodus 5:1, NASB. (8) Cf. Exodus 5:2. (9) Cf. Exodus 6:7. (10) Ephesians 4:29, 5:4; Colossians 3:8. (11) In *New International Dictionary of Old Testament Theology*, edited by Willem A. VanGemeren, vol. 1, ©1997 Willem A. VanGemeren, Zondervan Publishing House, Grand Rapids, Michigan. (12) Jeremiah 2:30, NASB. (13) Judges 2:10, NASB. (14) Hebrews 2:3, NASB. (15) Matthew 7:22, NASB. (16) Matthew 7:23, NASB.

Lawson G. Stone, Ph.D., is professor of Old Testament at Asbury Theological Seminary, in Wilmore, Kentucky. He and his wife, Angie, are parents of three children and live in Wilmore. ©2000 Billy Graham Evangelistic Association.

NOT TO BE TAKEN LIGHTLY

:: *BY H. CROSBY AND F.S. SCHENCK*

The literal rendering of the phrase, "To take in vain," is, "Thou shalt not lift up the name of Jehovah lightly." Taking God's name in vain is the flippant and thoughtless use of God's name. It is the taking up of His name in the vacant, purposeless way in which we pluck off a leaf as we pass along the road—the use of His name, not only where the purpose is evil, but where there is no defined purpose at all.

Beyond an absence of all purpose, there may even be a purpose of good, but this purpose may be seized upon in so rash and ill-advised a way that the use of the divine name in it is a taking of the name in vain, just as Uzzah's touching the Ark of God (2 Samuel 6:6–7), even to stay it upon the cart and prevent its fall, was a sin of profanity and called for the divine punishment.   —*H. Crosby*

The Third Commandment shows man at the head of the material creation with the crowning glory of intelligent speech and, as a social being, possessing the power of speech as the highest instrument of his social nature. God reveals Himself to man by word, by name, as to a speaking being, making language a bond of union between Himself and man.

God commands him to use this great gift in His worship, in honoring Him. The tongue is the glory of man, and the glory of the tongue is to voice the praises of God.

Man stands at the head of creation to take up its many notes of praise and to give them utterance. He stands thus not as a single individual, a great high priest, but as a race whose myriad voices are to join and mingle in a vast chorus of intelligent and harmonious praise. We are to speak of Him, and to Him, with adoration, love and praise. He is our Creator, Preserver, Governor and Judge. Our lips should quiver with emotion when we speak to Him in His worship, and of Him to each other, only in such a way as shall promote His worship in our own hearts and in the hearts of others.   *—F.S. Schenck*

These excerpts by H. Crosby and F.S. Schenck are taken from "Exodus," in *The Biblical Illustrator*, edited by Joseph S. Exell, published by Baker Book House Company, Grand Rapids, Michigan, in 1955.

FOUNDATIONS FOR LIFE
:: A CLOSER LOOK ::

The Third Commandment: *"You shall not take the name of the Lord your God in vain, for the Lord will not hold him guiltless who takes His name in vain"* (Exodus 20:7, NKJV).

OBSERVE

1. How is the name of God described?

Psalms 8:1, 52:9; Proverbs 18:10; Isaiah 63:14; Jeremiah 10:6

_____

_____

2. How does David describe those who misuse God's name?

Psalm 139:19–20 _____

_____

3. Several times in the Old Testament God's people turn their backs on Him, yet He does not cast them off. Why not?

1 Samuel 12:18–22_____

_____

Psalm 106:7–8 _____

_____

Ezekiel 36:17–38 _____

_____

4. How should we honor God's name?

Psalms 61:8, 86:9, 89:16, 92:1, 102:15, 119:55; Romans 15:9; Hebrews 2:12; Revelation 11:18_____

_____

_____

INTERPRET

1. Read how the priests in Malachi showed contempt for God's name. In what ways do we sometimes show contempt for God's name?

Malachi 1:6–8 _____

_____

_____

2. When Jeremiah said, *"Your words were found, and I ate them"* (Jeremiah 15:16, NKJV), he was speaking in figurative language about what he does, saying that he bears the Lord's name. In a practical sense, what does this mean?

Jeremiah 15:16 _____

_____

3. In what manner do biblical figures often appeal to God? Why do they do it in this way?

Joshua 7:8–9; Psalm 79:9; Jeremiah 14:7, 21; Daniel 9:19

_____

_____

APPLY

1. Think of your daily routine. What are some simple ways that you can bear God's name?

Colossians 3:17_____

_____

_____

REMEMBER THE SABBATH DAY, TO KEEP IT HOLY.

A DAY OF REST, A TIME FOR WORSHIP

:: *BY RONALD YOUNGBLOOD*

In 1967 Bethel Seminary, in St. Paul, Minnesota, granted me my first sabbatical leave from my responsibilities as an Old Testament professor. I decided to spend the year doing research in Israel.

After my wife, Carolyn; our children, Glenn and Wendy; and I arrived in Jerusalem, we began to look for a church home. We had enrolled Wendy in a Hebrew kindergarten where the children were required to attend from Sunday through Friday. The church that we chose, as far as we knew, was the only one in the entire city that held its weekly services on Saturday instead of on Sunday.

KEEPING THE SABBATH HOLY

For observant Jews throughout the world, including those in the land of Israel, the seventh day (Saturday) has been their day of rest and worship from the earliest times. Why have they always been so careful to keep their Sabbath day holy? A closer look at the Fourth Commandment and its context may help to answer that question.

A COVENANT SIGN

The Ten Commandments constitute the stipulations of the covenant that God made with His people at Mount Sinai. The sovereign Lord, who had redeemed the Israelites from Egyptian slavery, now demanded of them full obedience to His laws. On the basis of who He was (*"the Lord your God"*[1]), and on the basis of what He had done for them (*"brought you out of Egypt, out of the land of slavery*"[1]), God gave the Israelites 10 rules for living that they were to keep in perpetuity.

Because the covenant was a legal document, all of its stipulations had binding force. And the Fourth Commandment was considered to be so important among the Commandments that God mandated it as the covenant sign. Just as the rainbow was the sign of the Noahic covenant,[2] and just as circumcision was the sign of the Abrahamic covenant,[3] so also the Sabbath was to be the sign of the Mosaic covenant for all future generations.[4]

Throughout history, treaties and other covenants have often been broken shortly after being signed and witnessed. People tended to violate the treaties and covenants whenever they no longer served the purposes intended by the people.

Not so, however, with God. He has told us that He will never break His promises, that He is absolutely dependable and completely trustworthy, that He will never leave us nor forsake us.[5] God's Word is sure, and we can rely on it in all of life's circumstances.

But from our side, unfortunately, we frequently disobey God, even after we have signed on for the duration. How fickle is our behavior, how listless our worship, how shallow our faith! All that God asks of us, after all, is our obedience—not in order to be saved, but because we have already been saved. "I established My covenant with you,"[6] God said. *"I am the Lord your God, who brought you out of ... slavery."*[1] All He wants is our obedience—and at first we agree to give it to Him.[7]

Soon, however, we lapse into sin and attribute to alien gods the blessings that God has given us.[8] We forget that God requires very little of us[9] in comparison with the eternal benefits of the gracious covenant relationship we enjoy at His good hand.

A Shared Possession

The Sabbath day, Israel was told, was created by God and therefore belonged *"to the Lord your God."*[10] It was to be celebrated in His honor. He established it, He owned it, He consecrated it. The very first reference to the Sabbath in Scripture calls it *"a holy Sabbath to the Lord."*[11] Every Sabbath day belongs to Him. Each Sabbath is characterized as *"the Lord's holy day."*[12]

At the same time, however, God clearly stated that He has provided the Sabbath day for the blessing and benefit of His people. They are His Sabbaths, to be sure—but Jerusalem, even after she was destroyed, recognized that they were *"her Sabbaths"*[13] as well. The Lord has declared His willingness to share His day with us.

Jesus Himself pointed out that the Sabbath day was a possession jointly celebrated by God and His people. On one such day Jesus' disciples were picking some heads of grain, an act that drew criticism from a group of Pharisees.[14] Jesus used that incident to teach the Pharisees concerning what legitimate Sabbath-day activity is all about.

Jesus then said to them, *"The Sabbath was made for man, not man for the Sabbath. So the Son of Man is Lord even of the Sabbath."*[15] With one master stroke, Jesus underscored the truth that the Sabbath is a divine blessing for human benefit.

Needless to say, Jesus was not saying that Sabbath-day possession is shared equally by God and His people. Jesus is Lord not only of the Sabbath but also of us. His dominion over the Sabbath extends to all those who are blessed by it. So the Lord reserves to Himself the authority to decide how the Sabbath is to be used, when and why it is to be celebrated and who is to enjoy it.

A Day of Rest

"On it you shall not do any work. ... For in six days the Lord made the heavens and the earth, ... but he rested on the seventh day."[16] This characteristic of the Sabbath goes all the way back to the time of creation itself.

God's rest on the seventh day prefigured the establishment of a similar day of rest for His people. After six days of engaging in a series of majestic acts of creation, God "rested" from all His work.[17] The Hebrew verb translated "rested" is *shabat*, which is related to the noun rendered "Sabbath" (*shabbat*) throughout the Bible.

The "rest" implied by the word is not primarily the rest of relaxation. Rather, it is the rest of ceasing from work: *"In six days the Lord made the heavens and the earth, and on the seventh day he abstained from work and rested."*[18]

To work on the seventh day was so tempting and so despicable that prohibitions against all such activity were issued again and again. Engaging in any kind of business on that day was tantamount to "desecrating" it—that is, making it common or unholy.[19]

Although doing work on the Sabbath was forbidden, doing good on it was not thought of as violating the principle of rest. In fact, it was commended by Jesus Himself.[20] The Lord's holy day should therefore be looked upon as a source of blessing and an occasion for joy.[21]

Celebrating the Sabbath as a day of rest gave God's people an opportunity to benefit others as well: their servants, their farm animals, their guests.[22] It also reminded them that they had been slaves in Egypt and that the Lord had redeemed them from oppressive servitude by performing many and mighty acts of awesome power on their behalf.[23] That in itself was reason enough for them to *"remember the Sabbath day by keeping it holy."*[24]

A TIME FOR WORSHIP

The Sabbath is often listed along with other divinely ordained times as special occasions for worshiping the Lord. The three most common annual feasts were Unleavened Bread (preceded by Passover), Harvest or Weeks (Pentecost), and Ingathering or Tabernacles.[25] And the Sabbath day figured prominently not only in the weekly celebrations but in all the others as well.

The Bible says, *"The seventh day is a Sabbath of rest, a day of sacred assembly."*[26] It was looked forward to with a keen sense of excitement and anticipation. Leaving their six days of labor behind them, the people went to the tabernacle or temple or synagogue to worship the Lord in joyful assembly on the seventh day.

Worshiping in God's house on the Sabbath was the normal and customary practice of Jesus and His disciples.[27] Their example was emulated by the early Christians for decades following Jesus' death.[28]

The New Testament nowhere states that the first day of the week was celebrated in the early Church as a deliberate replacement for the Sabbath. On the other hand, Christians occasionally participated in various worship activities on the first day. These included the breaking of bread[29]—probably the Lord's Supper—and the bringing of monetary offerings.[30] In any event, many aspects of Sabbath rest and worship eventually became part and parcel of Sunday celebration in the lives of Christians the world over.

Why then do the Christians at the church that we attended in Jerusalem worship on Saturdays instead of Sundays? The answer to that question may be simple: Most of their non-Christian neighbors work from Sunday through Friday. So if the church members want to invite their Israeli neighbors to join them in worship, they must schedule their services for Saturday. The end result is a small but dedicated and growing number of Jewish believers who have placed their faith in Christ as their Savior.

It is my prayer that we too will be discerning and creative in our choices of when and how we keep our Sabbaths holy.

---

(1) Exodus 20:2, NIV. (2) Genesis 9:13. (3) Genesis 17:11. (4) Exodus 31:13, 16–17; Ezekiel 20:12, 20. (5) Joshua 1:5; Hebrews 13:5. (6) Cf. Genesis 9:11. (7) Exodus 19:8; 24:3, 7. (8) Exodus 32:3–4. (9) Micah 6:8. (10) Exodus 20:10, NIV. (11) Exodus 16:23, NIV. (12) Isaiah 58:13, NIV. (13) Lamentations 2:6, NIV. (14) Mark 2:23–24. (15) Mark 2:27–28, NIV. (16) Exodus 20:10–11, NIV. (17) Genesis 2:2–3. (18) Exodus 31:17, NIV. (19) Exodus 31:14. (20) Matthew 12:11–12; Mark 3:2–4. (21) Genesis 2:3; Exodus 20:11. (22) Exodus 20:10; Deuteronomy 5:14. (23) Deuteronomy 5:15. (24) Exodus 20:8, NIV. (25) Exodus 23:14–17. (26) Leviticus 23:3, NIV. (27) Mark 1:21; 3:1–2; 6:1–2. (28) Acts 13:14–15; 17:1–4; 18:4. (29) Acts 20:7. (30) 1 Corinthians 16:2.

Ronald Youngblood, Ph.D., is professor of Old Testament at International College and Graduate School in Honolulu, Hawaii. He is the author and editor of numerous books. He and his wife, Carolyn, are parents of two grown children. ©2000 Billy Graham Evangelistic Association.

DON'T FORGET GOD

:: *BY CLOVIS G. CHAPPELL*

How are we to use Sunday? It is to be a day of rest, and it is to be a day that offers opportunity for worship. The highest use of Sunday, and far the most rewarding, is to make it a day of worship and rest. Worship and rest, these two go together. When we cease to worship, the pull of the world is likely to rob us of our day of rest. When we cease to rest, we are likely to cease to worship.

Everyone needs this holy day. We cannot manage life without it. Life is too hectic for most of us. Just as universal as our need for rest is our need for worship. To worship aright, we need time.

When we forget this day, we are on the way to forgetting God. Therefore, not as an end, but as a means to the high end of being and doing our best, we ought to remember the Sabbath to keep it holy.

This article is taken from *Ten Rules for Living*, by Clovis G. Chappell, ©1938 Whitmore and Smith, Abingdon Press, Nashville, Tennessee.

FOUNDATIONS FOR LIFE
:: A CLOSER LOOK ::

The Fourth Commandment: *"Remember the Sabbath day, to keep it holy. Six days you shall labor and do all your work, but the seventh day is the Sabbath of the Lord your God. In it you shall do no work: you, nor your son, nor your daughter, nor your male servant, nor your female servant, nor your cattle, nor your stranger who is within your gates. For in six days the Lord made the heavens and the earth, the sea, and all that is in them, and rested the seventh day. Therefore the Lord blessed the Sabbath day and hallowed it"* (Exodus 20:8–11, NKJV).

OBSERVE

1. Read Exodus 20:8–11. Then read Exodus 23:12. What reasons are given for keeping the Sabbath? _____

_____

_____

_____

2. What was the penalty for not keeping the Sabbath?
Exodus 35:1–3 _____

_____

_____

_____

3. What did Jesus and His disciples do on the Sabbath that angered the Pharisees? How did Jesus respond to the Pharisees?
Matthew 12:1–14 _____

_____

_____

_____

INTERPRET

1. What does it mean not to go your own way and not do as you please on the Sabbath? What is the result of honoring the Sabbath?

Isaiah 58:13–14 _____

_____

_____

2. What does it really mean to keep the Sabbath holy? Does this Commandment suggest that certain things are allowed on the Sabbath but others are not? _____

_____

_____

3. What is the context of the Apostle Paul's statement: "Do not let anyone judge you with regard to a Sabbath day" (cf. Colossians 2:16)? What lesson is Paul trying to teach in this passage?

Colossians 2:6–23 _____

_____

_____

APPLY

1. Taking into account both the Old Testament and the New Testament teachings on the Sabbath, examine your own life. Write down ways in which you can bring your life into accordance with God's will regarding the Sabbath.

_____

_____

_____

_____

HONOR YOUR FATHER AND YOUR MOTHER.

HOW DO WE HONOR OUR PARENTS?

:: *BY DAVID A. DORSEY*

As usual, I was wrong.

It was 1976, and Jan and I had been married for four years. I was completing my graduate studies, and Jan was taking care of our two small sons at home. One day between diaper changes Jan read in Genesis the story of Joseph. She came to God's promise to the elderly Jacob: *"Do not be afraid to go down to Egypt, for ... I will go down to Egypt with you. ... And Joseph's own hand will close your eyes."*[1]

Jan was deeply touched by the image of Joseph caring for his aging father and closing his father's eyes when he died. She decided to pray that God would give her the privilege of caring for her own parents in their later years.

I pointed out to Jan that this was probably not going to happen, because she was the fourth of six children, and some of her older siblings were more settled than we were, and they were far more likely than we to be the ones to support Mom and Dad as they grew older.

As I said, I was wrong.

Jan's prayer was answered several years later when her dad and mom retired and decided to come and live with us. The four of us designed an extension to our house—a separate, independently functioning apartment that was connected to the main part of our house by a shared garage.

We all enjoyed the new arrangement. Mom and Dad had their own lives and activities, and at the same time Jan and I were next door to give a hand if needed. We did many things together—and we did many things separately.

When Dad's health began to deteriorate because of Parkinson's disease, Jan became more involved in helping her parents. Dad's condition worsened considerably during his final two years, and Jan and her mom devoted more and more time to caring for him. Dad remained at home until two weeks before he died.

It has been about three years since Dad passed away. Jan continues to help and to enjoy the companionship of her mom, who is now in her eighties. Mom usually comes over for coffee in the morning and joins us for dinner every night. Although she still has her own life and friends, Mom does more things with us now. She and Jan shop together, can tomatoes together, and often plan and prepare meals together.

As Christians, we are familiar with the Fifth Commandment, *"Honor your father and your mother,"*[2] and Jan's support of her parents has been part of her commitment to honor them. We know that honoring parents is important to God, because He included a Commandment requiring it among His 10 most basic stipulations for Israel. Indeed, this Fifth Commandment is the only one with a motivational promise: *"so that you may live long in the land the Lord your God is giving you."*[2] The honoring of parents was so important that God would not allow His people to live in the Promised Land if they failed to do it.

PRIMARILY FOR ADULTS

Parents often quote the Fifth Commandment to their children and teenagers as an incentive to obedience, and certainly the Commandment has implications for minors. But the Commandment is primarily for adults, not children. Adults are the understood recipients of all the Ten Commandments.

This is seen, for example, in the Fourth Commandment, which prohibits making one's sons or daughters work on the Sabbath[3]; and the Tenth Commandment, which forbids coveting a neighbor's wife or servant.[4] The Fifth Commandment declares that adults are to honor their (aging) parents. This is how Jesus understood this Commandment, as shown by His words to the Pharisees: *"Why do you break the command of God for the sake of your tradition? For God said,*

'Honor your father and mother.' ... But you say that if a man says to his father or mother, 'Whatever help you might otherwise have received from me is a gift devoted to God,' he is not to 'honor his father' with it. Thus you nullify the word of God for the sake of your tradition."[5]

The social reality in any culture is that parents, as they age, become less and less "useful" to their children. Aging parents gradually need more help because of physical weakening, illnesses, loss of physical functions, loss of income or loss of a spouse. The tendency of human beings is to devalue that which has little tangible use to them.

Indeed, the Bible is full of examples of children dishonoring their aging parents, such as Ham's shameful treatment of his father, Noah[6]; Jacob's deception of his blind father, Isaac[7]; and the disrespect that Hophni and Phinehas showed their elderly father, Eli.[8] The Fifth Commandment declares that this human tendency is to be reversed: God's people are to honor their aging parents.

THE MEANING OF "HONOR"

What exactly does it mean to "honor" one's father and mother? The Hebrew word used in this command is *kabbed*, which comes from a root word that means "heavy, weighty." The verb could be translated as "treat as weighty or important." That verb is used in the Old Testament in five ways:

1. **To honor a person by showing him respect, by treating him with dignity, by acting toward him as one would toward an important person.** Saul, for example, when he had been humiliated by Samuel's announcement that Saul was rejected by God, pled with Samuel to honor him publicly by accompanying him back to his capital.[9]

2. **To honor a person by verbally expressing one's respect or esteem for that person.** In Isaiah we read that God said, *"These people ... honor me with their lips, but their hearts are far from me."*[10]

3. **To honor a person by behaving in a way that shows respect for the other person's principles and values.**

Israel, for example, was to honor God by observing the Sabbath.[11]

4. **To honor a person by giving to him financially.** The writer of Proverbs exhorted, *"Honor the Lord with your wealth, with the firstfruits of all your crops."*[12]

5. **To honor a person by elevating him to a position of respect and esteem.** The writer of Proverbs declared, *"Esteem [wisdom], and she will exalt you; embrace her, and she will honor you."*[13]

The Commandment to honor one's parents undoubtedly includes all these meanings.

APPLICABILITY TO CHRISTIANS

The Fifth Commandment reveals insights about God's heart and mind that should profoundly affect our behavior as Christians. It reveals that God cares about the plight of aging parents. It shows that God considers aging parents worthy of honor—mothers as well as fathers (a surprise, considering Israel's patriarchal world). It also shows that God wants His people to reflect these values by honoring their aging parents.

How should we respond to this Commandment in our own lives? As already suggested, we can begin by showing respect to our parents, treating them as important and supporting them financially or otherwise as needed. But beyond these generalities, what specific things can we do to honor our parents?

There are hundreds of ways that we can honor our parents: visiting them, taking trips with them, inviting them to our homes for the weekend, asking them about their lives, doing odd jobs for them, giving them financial assistance, and, in some cases, having them move in with us.

I heard of a woman who recently retired from teaching and devoted her first year of retirement to her mother. For an entire year she spent time with her mother. They traveled around the world together, and they did many other activities together. They came to know each other better than ever, and it is likely that the mother felt honored by her daughter.

When my dad was 70 years old, we took a car trip together to retrace his early years. During this trip "down memory lane," he and I visited little towns in the hills of West Virginia and met childhood friends that Daddy had not seen in more than 55 years.

I heard many stories about my dad's life, stories that I will always treasure. We both enjoyed the experience, and I am sure that Daddy was honored by it.

We should treat our parents as we would like to be treated someday by our own children. Because each person's circumstance is different, we should not make generalities, such as, "No one should put his or her parents into a retirement home." God is the best guide for how we should honor our own parents.

What about cases where a parent is an alcoholic, or is emotionally absent, or is extremely difficult or even wicked—a physical or sexual abuser? How can God expect His children to honor such parents?

In cases like these, one should seek God's own mind and the advice of wise friends or a counselor. Perhaps honoring might mean confronting the parent and holding him or her accountable for past destructive behavior. Perhaps honoring such a parent is possible only from a safe distance, through letters or cards. Perhaps all that is possible, or advisable, is to pray faithfully for the parent. Here again, God is the best guide for how to apply the Fifth Commandment in such difficult circumstances.

And what about those whose parents are no longer living? Because the Fifth Commandment assumes that elderly people are highly valued by God, the Commandment has implications for our treatment of all elderly people, not just our parents. If we have lost our own parents (and even if we haven't!), we should respond to this Commandment by showing honor and love to any elderly person—the elderly woman down the street, or an aging aunt or uncle.

Whatever our circumstances, one thing is certain. When we sincerely seek to fulfill the Commandment to honor our parents, we also honor and delight our heavenly Father by our obedience.

(1) Genesis 46:3–4, NIV. (2) Exodus 20:12, NIV. (3) Exodus 20:10. (4) Exodus 20:17. (5) Matthew 15:3–6, NIV. (6) Genesis 9:20–23. (7) Genesis 27. (8) 1 Samuel 2:22–25. (9) 1 Samuel 15:30. (10) Isaiah 29:13, NIV. (11) Isaiah 58:13. (12) Proverbs 3:9, NIV. (13) Proverbs 4:8, NIV.

David A. Dorsey, Ph.D., is professor of Old Testament at Evangelical School of Theology, in Myerstown, Pennsylvania. He and his wife, Janet, are parents of three grown children and live in Myerstown. ©2000 Billy Graham Evangelistic Association.

TREAT YOUR PARENTS WITH HONOR

:: BY D.L. MOODY

If your parents are still living, treat them kindly. Do all you can to make their declining years sweet and happy. Bear in mind that this is the only Commandment that you may not always be able to obey because the day comes to most people when father and mother die. What bitter feelings you will have when the opportunity has gone by if you fail to show them the respect and love that is their due!

Come, are you ready to be weighed? If you have been dishonoring your father and mother, step into the scales and see how quickly you will be found wanting. See how quickly you will strike the beam. I don't know any person who is much lighter than the one who treats his parents with contempt.

You may be a professing Christian, but I wouldn't give much for your religion unless it gets into your life and teaches you how to live. I wouldn't give a snap of my finger for a religion that doesn't begin at home and doesn't regulate conduct toward parents.

D.L. Moody (1837–1899) was a well-known itinerant urban evangelist and a noted educator. In 1886 he founded the first Bible school of its kind in the United States, the Chicago Evangelization Society, later known as the Moody Bible Institute. He conducted evangelistic campaigns throughout the United States, England, Ireland and Scotland. This excerpt is taken from *Weighed and Wanting: Addresses on the Ten Commandments*, by D.L. Moody, published by Moody Press, Chicago, Illinois.

FOUNDATIONS FOR LIFE
:: A CLOSER LOOK ::

The Fifth Commandment: *"Honor your father and your mother, that your days may be long upon the land which the Lord your God is giving you"* (Exodus 20:12, NKJV).

OBSERVE

1. The Fifth Commandment is initially given in Exodus 20:12, and it is repeated by Moses to a new generation in Deuteronomy 5:16. Compare these two passages. How does the Deuteronomy passage expand on the Exodus passage?

_____

_____

2. The book of Ruth tells the story of the support that Ruth gave to her aging mother-in-law, Naomi. Read this brief book and list 10 ways that Ruth honored and supported her mother-in-law.

_____

_____

_____

_____

INTERPRET

1. The Fifth Commandment says, *"Honor your father* and your mother *[emphasis added]"* (Exodus 20:12, NKJV). The ancient Middle East was a patriarchal world in which women had few rights and were accorded little respect. What does this Commandment suggest about God's view of the value of women?

_____

_____

2. The Apostle Paul addresses children directly in Ephesians 6:1–3. What does Paul tell children to do? How do you differentiate between obeying your parents and honoring your parents?

_____

_____

_____

_____

APPLY

1. Even if you and your parents have had a difficult relationship, list three things that you respect or admire about them.

_____

_____

_____

2. Think of the way you have treated your parents, and list three ways in which you will honor them during each week this month.

_____

_____

_____

3. Read the Apostle Paul's strong words about caring for the needs of one's family, in 1 Timothy 5:3–8. How will you put your religion into practice?

_____

_____

_____

You shall not murder.

WHERE "MURDER" BEGINS

:: *BY ALEX LUC*

Murder was merely a remote and theoretical matter to me until a spring night several years ago. I was attending a high school drama with my two teen-aged sons. The play lasted longer than it was originally scheduled, so during the intermission, my sons and I went out to the side of the school to call home. My wife was ill that night, and I wanted to let her know our situation.

Though not far from the school, the public telephone was in a dimly lit area. I hung up the telephone receiver and turned around to see two young men pointing guns at my head. The "click-click" sounded so loud in the darkness that I knew they were willing to kill.

One of my sons had slipped away to call for help and my other son told the robbers, "Don't shoot!" The robbers took my wallet and ran even before looking in it.

During the incident, the words of Psalm 23, *"You are with me,"*[1] became especially real to me. Earlier that day, I had taught this psalm to a class.

Stories like mine, and much worse stories that have happened to other people, are many. Our society needs to hear again the thundering voice of the Author of life, *"You shall not murder."*[2]

THE MEANING OF "MURDER"

Though the Hebrew word for "murder" (*rāsah*) in the Sixth Commandment occurs in some contexts of unintentional killing, its usage essentially has to do with premeditated murder. This usage is affirmed by the fact that its uses require no modification from words of intentionality, while in cases referring to unintentional killing, words such as "by mistake" or "not knowingly" are added for clarification.[3]

In the Old Testament the word never refers to the act of killing by an animal, a meaning we see in the term *hēmît*.[4] The latter term has a broad usage, including frequent references to capital punishment.[5]

Another term *hārag* ("kill") also broadly covers premeditated killing and capital punishment.[6] These two terms are sometimes used to refer to God's punishing of people with death, a usage never found in the term *rāsah* of the Sixth Commandment.[7]

THE COMMANDMENT AND THE OLD TESTAMENT

An important background passage for the Sixth Commandment is Genesis 9:6, in which God proclaimed, *"Whoever sheds the blood of man, by man shall his blood be shed; for God made man in his own image."*[8] The idiom "shedding blood" is synonymous with "murder" and occurs almost as frequently. This proclamation explains the evil of taking the life of a person.

Murder is not only against the victim but against God, because each human being is made in the image of God. This understanding also encompasses the universal application of the Sixth Commandment and capital punishment for murderers in Old Testament laws.

The book of Exodus, the immediate context of the Sixth Commandment, continues the theme of salvation begun in Genesis: God has called and preserved a people to be His channel of blessing for all the families of the earth. Exodus begins with the midwives' refusal to murder the male babies of the Hebrews.

In the context of Exodus, the Sixth Commandment's emphasis on preserving life contributes an important part to the theme of salvation. The Old Testament solemnly warns that bloodshed pollutes the land and commands that "a murderer must be put to death."[9]

The concern for human life was the main reason behind God's command to establish the cities of refuge. It is God's will that any one who unintentionally kills another person may not needlessly die by the hand of *"the avenger of blood."*[10] The establishment of the cities of refuge allows that "a slayer may not die until a trial before the congregation."[11]

This concern for human life in the Sixth Commandment is reflected in a number of subsequent Old Testament laws. Two examples are warnings against possessing animals dangerous to humans and building a house without a parapet.[12]

The book of Proverbs begins by warning youth not to give in to material temptation to join peers to commit murder, a warning pointing to where murder often begins: a greedy heart.[13]

In the prophetic books the oppression of the poor among God's people is frequently described as murder. Isaiah charges that the hands of the oppressors are *"full of blood,"*[14] and that the society as a whole is covered with bloodshed. As a result, the destruction of the people, including the oppressors, becomes inevitable.[15] Similarly, Ezekiel announces that the end of Jerusalem has come because the city is "shedding blood within itself."[16]

If murder is wrong, what about Israel's killing of their enemies in wars commanded by God? First, the Commandment does not directly address the issue of war. Second, wars are not glorified in the Old Testament. Wars were inevitable for a people attempting to survive in a hostile environment, but many Old Testament passages reflect God's desire that His people will cease engaging in wars.

In Isaiah we read that God announced that *"nation shall not lift up sword against nation, neither shall they learn war any more."*[17] When Israel's longtime enemy, Moab, fell victim to war, Isaiah said that God's heart ached for them. Moreover, God proclaims that Israel will one day worship together with the Egyptians and the Assyrians. And the Egyptians will be called by God as *"my people"*[18] and the Assyrians as *"the work of my hands."*[18] No war today may claim to be supported by divine revelation as were the wars of the Old Testament.

THE COMMANDMENT AND JESUS

Contrary to how the people of ancient times have interpreted the Sixth Commandment, Jesus includes anger and insult as violations.[19] This does not mean that Jesus teaches that there is no difference between these and actual killing, but that a proper understanding of the Commandment needs to include them.

Jesus' understanding has support from the Pentateuch. The Sixth Commandment has an important context: the Ten Commandments. The context begins and ends with Commandments that point directly to the heart, the place where God's words ultimately apply. Both the First Commandment, *"You shall have no other gods before me,"*[20] and the Tenth Commandment, *"You shall not covet,"*[21] call for the devotion of our hearts. This demand on our inward attitude is expected in the teaching of Deuteronomy 6:4–6, one of the foundational passages for ancient Israel: *"Hear, O Israel: ... Love the Lord your God with all your heart. ... These commandments ... are to be upon your hearts."*[22]

Any understanding of God's Commandments that ignores the role of the human heart is an incomplete understanding. In linking the Commandment to the human heart, Jesus pointed to the source of the violation; in so doing He helps us to see the full intent of the Commandment. As He also said, *"For out of the heart come evil thoughts, murder."*[23]

THE COMMANDMENT AND US

Our society has continued to witness horrible acts of violence. Added to this list are abortion, euthanasia, suicide, hate crimes, racism. We as a society have continued to devalue human life. Entertained by the violence in the media, we are being numbed.

Is there hope? Yes. God continues to preserve a people who will make a difference in this world. The Ten Commandments were given to a generation who lived through violence and who murmured for self-fulfillment. The hope lies in bringing people to a relationship with the true God. All Commandments will have little impact on our lives if they are not seen as presupposing a relationship with God, as shown by the early part of the Ten Commandments.[24]

Government intervention and interventions by various social and religious institutions may reduce some violent incidences, but the real change can come only when people forsake their idols to worship God. When our idol is physical power, violence may be the solution to life's problems. When our idol is self-fulfillment, abortion may become a convenience.

The Sixth Commandment also possesses implications beyond the obvious. In view of Jesus' teaching, we need to see in a new light our anger and our insults against others, for these have the effect of destroying lives. To obey the Sixth Commandment is in a sense to see every human being as God sees him or her—as precious.

---

(1) Psalm 23:4, NIV. (2) Exodus 20:13, NIV. (3) Numbers 25:11; Deuteronomy 4:42; Deuteronomy 19:4; Joshua 20:3, 5. (4) Exodus 21:29. (5) Leviticus 20:4; Numbers 35:19, 21; Deuteronomy 13:10; Deuteronomy 17:7. (6) Genesis 4:8; Exodus 21:14; Leviticus 20:16; Numbers 25:5. (7) For *hēmit*: Genesis 38:7; Numbers 14:15; for *hārag*: Genesis 20:4; Exodus 4:23. (8) Genesis 9:6, RSV. (9) Cf. Numbers 35:16. (10) Numbers 35:24, NIV. (11) Cf. Numbers 35:12, 25; cf. Deuteronomy 4:42. (12) Exodus 21:29–32; Deuteronomy 22:8. (13) Proverbs 1:10–19. (14) Isaiah 1:15, RSV. (15) Isaiah 1:15–17; Isaiah 5:7, 13. (16) Cf. Ezekiel 22:3–5. (17) Isaiah 2:4, RSV. (18) Isaiah 19:25, RSV. (19) Matthew 5:21–24. (20) Exodus 20:3, NIV. (21) Exodus 20:17, NIV. (22) Deuteronomy 6:4–6, NIV. (23) Matthew 15:19, NIV. (24) Exodus 20:2–4.

Alex Luc, Ph.D., is professor of Old Testament and Semitic languages at Columbia International University, in Columbia, South Carolina. He and his wife, Trina, are parents of two children. ©2000 Billy Graham Evangelistic Association.

WHO HAS THE RIGHT TO END LIFE?

:: *BY G. CAMPBELL MORGAN*

At the very foundation of social fabric is the sovereignty of God that is over every individual life. Human life is emphatically declared to be sacred. It is a divine creation, mysterious and magnificent in its genesis and possibility, utterly beyond the control or comprehension of any human being. It is, therefore, never to be taken at the will of one who can by no means know the full meaning of its being.

The revelation of God made to man proves that He has purposes for every individual and for the human race, stretching far beyond the present moment or manifestation. To terminate a single life is to set up the wit and wisdom of man as superior to that of God.

The immensity of the issues of death is so great that there can be no sin against humanity, and therefore against God, that is greater than that of taking life. In this brief Commandment is contained a statement of the first principle of human life, so clear and so vital as to demand the closest attention.

Life, being a gift of God, is in itself the most wonderful relationship, that of man to God. This Commandment, therefore, in simplest words, and yet in sternest manner, flings a fiery Law around the life of every human being, reserving to Him who first bestowed it the right to end it.

G. Campbell Morgan (1863–1945) was a British Congregational minister. A lecturer and a Bible teacher, he traveled widely in the United States and in Canada in evangelistic and preaching missions. He was the author of 60 books and a dozen booklets. This message was taken from *The Ten Commandments*, by G. Campbell Morgan, ©1901 The Bible Institute Colportage Association of Chicago, Fleming H. Revell Company, a division of Baker Book House Company, Grand Rapids, Michigan; used by permission of the Reverend G. Campbell Morgan Estate, London, England.

FOUNDATIONS FOR LIFE
:: A CLOSER LOOK ::

The Sixth Commandment: *"You shall not murder"* (Exodus 20:13, NKJV).

OBSERVE

1. Proverbs 1:10–19 teaches us three things about murder. According to the passage, what is one motive for murder? What consequences will an offender face? What are we instructed to avoid?

Proverbs 1:13–14 _____

_____

_____

Proverbs 1:17–19 _____

_____

_____

Proverbs 1:10, 15 _____

_____

_____

2. How does Jesus interpret the Sixth Commandment?

Matthew 5:21–22 _____

_____

_____

3. What allowance did God make for Israelites who killed someone accidentally?

Numbers 35:9–13 _____

_____

_____

INTERPRET

1. Explain why Jesus' teaching on the Sixth Commandment, in Matthew 5:21–22, is not a correction of the Old Testament but a clarification of its divine intent.

Matthew 5:17–20 _____

_____

Matthew 15:19 _____

_____

2. Murder is a violation against the victim. Why is it also a violation against God?

Genesis 9:6 _____

_____

Psalm 139:13–16 _____

_____

APPLY

1. What are the implications of the Sixth Commandment in light of Jesus' teaching? Name one specific action that you need to take to be obedient to this Commandment.

Matthew 5:21–25 _____

_____

2. Now name one specific action that you need to take in order to restore your relationship with God.

1 John 1:9_____

_____

3. What comfort do you find in Psalm 103:8–13?

_____

_____

You shall not commit adultery.

ADULTERY—BETRAYED COMMITMENTS

:: *BY TREMPER LONGMAN III*

"Having an affair? I can't believe it!" I had cried out when my minister told me about John and Marty. But it was true. Two leaders in our church had betrayed the commitments that they had made to their spouses and had been caught carrying on a secret intimate relationship.

In one sense, I should not have been surprised. After all, probably every Christian knows of situations like this one. Perhaps the vehemence of my response was connected more to the consequences that I knew would follow.

Adultery devastates relationships, and not just the relationship of the two couples most directly involved. My thoughts went to their teen-aged children. What would happen to them? And the parents of both John and Marty—they would be heartbroken. And the church!

The relational damage spread far and wide, and the next two years brought tears, pain, conflict and division in our church and in the personal lives of John and Marty.

Adultery involves a fundamental betrayal of the most intimate of all human relationships. God instituted marriage soon after the creation of the first human being, Adam. Among the creatures, man did not at first have a partner who was his equal, his soulmate. So God created the woman Eve. She was even created from the very body of Adam, according to Genesis 2:21–22. Adam and Eve were two separate individuals, but they belonged naturally together. Adam expressed this in the first poem in the Bible: *"This is now bone of my bones and flesh of my flesh; she shall be called 'woman,' for she was taken out of man."*[1]

Marriage is God's good gift to us and the boundary within which we may enjoy sexual intercourse. Sex is more than a physical thing; it binds two people into a close psychological and spiritual unity. By prohibiting extramarital sex, God is protecting our most intimate human relationships.

And according to Jesus, to observe the Seventh Commandment means more than refraining from physical touch. Jesus gets to the heart of the prohibition when He said that *"anyone who looks at a woman lustfully has already committed adultery with her in his heart."*[2] The stringency of Christ's statement indicates that few of us are completely without sin in this area. Christ's Sermon on the Mount[3] shows us that it is not only our outward actions that are sinful, but it is also our inner attitudes in our hearts that cause us to fall short of God's plans and necessitate God's forgiveness.

THE CELEBRATION OF SEXUALITY

God shows the importance of the marriage relationship by giving us the Seventh Commandment, which prohibits sexual relationships outside the marriage bond. Sex is more than a physical act. It enhances the relationship of a couple beyond the physical to include psychological and spiritual oneness.

However, though the prohibition is clear, we must not think that the Commandment against adultery simply prohibits sexual intercourse outside marriage. As with all the Commandments, the prohibition against adultery also has a positive side. It encourages a celebration of sexuality within marriage.

Some people think that the Bible is anti-sex, but this viewpoint is wrong. The Bible prohibits sexual relationships outside marriage but celebrates God's good gift of sexuality within marriage, between husband and wife. In becoming *"one flesh"*[4] Adam and Eve became the model for all later marriages. The unity of marriage partners involves more than physical union, but Christians sometimes make the mistake of separating the physical from the spiritual aspects of the relationship. Physical intimacy is very important in marriage.

In the garden Adam and Eve were *"both naked, and they felt no shame."*[5] They were completely vulnerable to one another, physically, psychologically and spiritually. The alienation between Adam and Eve that resulted because of their rebellion against God is apparent in that they could no longer stand naked in each other's presence without embarrassment. They covered themselves and hid from God.

However, with God redemption is possible, even in the area of devastated marital relationships—the Bible's positive attitude is clear in the Song of Songs. This book is a collection of love poems where the unnamed man and the unnamed woman revel in one another, particularly in terms of physical attraction.

Consider the expression of love in Song of Songs 8:6–7: *"Place me like a seal over your heart, like a seal on your arm; for love is as strong as death, its jealousy unyielding as the grave. It burns like blazing fire, like a mighty flame. Many waters cannot quench love; rivers cannot wash it away."*[6]

Love is as strong as death. Love is powerful and to be desired. The woman wants the man to place her like a seal on his arm. That seal was like a stamp with a form of personal identification; it acted like a signature, marking identity and ownership. The Song of Songs is an example in the Bible of the importance of marital love and physical intimacy.

A PARALLEL RELATIONSHIP

The marriage relationship is unique in that it is the human relationship that most clearly parallels our relationship with God. Marriage is the only human relationship that demands exclusive fidelity. Other relationships, even close ones, do not. We can have more than one friend, more than one child, more than one parent, more than one business associate and so on. But we can have only one spouse.

Marriage is also the only relationship where jealousy may be a virtue. Jealousy is a passion to keep someone for oneself and allow no other to threaten the relationship. Notice in Song of Songs 8:6 that jealousy is spoken of positively in parallel to love. Now, jealousy is not always a right attitude in marriage. There is unfounded jealousy and abusive jealousy, but within marriage appropriate jealousy can possibly save a relationship.

Marty's husband Ralph later told me that before he found out about the affair between his wife and John, he was jealous that she was spending so much time with him. But he said that he believed jealousy to be wrong and that God would not want him to feel such a negative emotion. Ralph came to regret that he hadn't acted on his jealousy, moving in appropriate ways to save his relationship with his wife.

Marriage relationships and our relationship with God are exclusive relationships. We can have only one God, as we can have only one spouse. This truth is clear in the Old Testament, and in the New Testament Ephesians 5:22–33 explicitly likens the relationship between Jesus Christ and the Church to the relationship between husband and wife.

Similarly, in the Bible a broken relationship with God is compared to a broken marriage. Hosea 1–3 is a vivid illustration of the relationship that God had with His rebellious people Israel. God directed the Prophet Hosea to marry a prostitute to illustrate that when Israel rejected her Husband, God grew jealous and fought to get His bride back.

The first two Commandments and the Seventh Commandment have a special relationship. Idolatry, worshiping any god other than the Lord God, is spiritual adultery. It is not surprising that in the context of the Second Commandment God describes Himself as a *"jealous God."*[7] In the same way, when people break the Seventh Commandment, they sin against God and also are breaking the first two Commandments.

God wants the best for His people, and He knows that we don't always understand what that is. John and Marty thought that they were in love with each other, even though they were already married to other people. They listened to their desires rather than to God's wisdom in the Seventh Commandment. Now, years later, John and Marty are still dealing with the fallout of damaged careers and destroyed relationships.

Even in the most severe cases, redemption is possible, but divine forgiveness does not mean that the consequences of betrayal will immediately go away. God knows what is best, and what is best is that sex be reserved for marriage, the relationship of exclusive commitment.

---

(1) Genesis 2:23, NIV. (2) Matthew 5:28, NIV. (3) Matthew 5–7. (4) Genesis 2:24, NIV. (5) Genesis 2:25, NIV. (6) Song of Songs 8:6–7, NIV. (7) Exodus 20:5, NIV.

Tremper Longman III, Ph.D., is the Robert H. Gundry professor of biblical studies at Westmont College, in Santa Barbara, California. He and his wife, Alice, are parents of three children. ©2000 Billy Graham Evangelistic Association.

10 WAYS TO AVOID ADULTERY

:: BY THOMAS WATSON

In the late 1600s Thomas Watson wrote giving practical advice for avoiding the temptation to commit adultery. Today, 300 years later, his suggestions are still practical.

Here are some directions to keep from the infection of adultery:

1. **Look to your eyes.** The eye tempts the fancy, and the fancy works upon the heart. Eve first saw the tree of knowledge, and then she took.[1] The eye often sets the heart on fire.

2. **Look to your lips.** Take heed of any unseemly word that may kindle unclean thoughts in you or others: *"Set a watch, O Lord, before my mouth."*[2]

3. **Look to your heart:** *"Out of the heart proceed evil thoughts."*[3] Thinking of sin makes way for the act of sin. Suppress the first risings of sin in your heart.

4. **Take heed of lascivious books and pictures that provoke lust.** The reading of the Scripture stirs up love to God, and the reading of unclean material stirs up the mind to wickedness.

5. **Take heed of idleness.** When a person is idle, he is ready to receive any temptation. When David was idle on the top of his house, he espied Bathsheba and took her to him.[4]

6. **To avoid adultery every man should have a chaste love for his wife.** Solomon prescribed a remedy against adultery: *"Rejoice with the wife of thy youth."*[5] It is not having a wife, but loving a wife, that makes a man live chastely. Pure love is a gift of God, and it comes from heaven; but, like the vestal fire, it must be cherished that it go not out.

7. **Labor to get the fear of God into your hearts:** *"By the fear of the Lord men depart from evil."*[6] How did Joseph keep from temptation? The fear of God pulled him back: *"How then can I do this great wickedness, and sin against God?"*[7]

8. **Take delight in the Word of God:** *"How sweet are thy words unto my taste!"*[8] He who has tasted Christ in a promise is ravished with delight. How would he scorn a motion to sin!

9. **If you would abstain from adultery, use serious consideration.** Consider that God sees you in the act of sin. He is both witness and judge. Few who are entangled in adultery recover from the snare: *"None that go unto her return again."*[9] ... *"The lips of a strange woman drop as an honeycomb, ... But her end is bitter as wormwood."*[10] When the senses have feasted on unchaste pleasures, the soul is left to pay the reckoning.

10. **Pray against this sin.** When lust begins to rise in your heart, go to prayer. Prayer is the best armor to quench the wildfire of lust. If prayer will *"cast out devils,"*[11] why may it not cast out lusts from the devil?

---

(1) Genesis 3:6. (2) Psalm 141:3, KJV. (3) Matthew 15:19, KJV. (4) 2 Samuel 11:1–4. (5) Proverbs 5:18, KJV. (6) Proverbs 16:6, KJV. (7) Genesis 39:9, KJV. (8) Psalm 119:103, KJV. (9) Proverbs 2:19, KJV. (10) Proverbs 5:3–4, KJV. (11) Mark 16:17, KJV.

Thomas Watson (c.1620–c.1686) was a Puritan preacher and an author in London, England. He was graduated from Emmanuel College, University of Cambridge, in Cambridge. He is the author of *Body of Divinity*, *The Ten Commandments* and *The Lord's Prayer*, which are based on the Westminster Shorter Catechism. This article is taken from *The Ten Commandments*, by Thomas Watson, first published as part of *A Body of Practical Divinity* in 1692, reprinted in 1890, reprinted in 1959 by The Banner of Truth Trust, London, England, 1965.

FOUNDATIONS FOR LIFE
:: A CLOSER LOOK ::

The Seventh Commandment: *"You shall not commit adultery"* (Exodus 20:14, NKJV).

OBSERVE

1. In the New Testament, what does Jesus Christ say about the sin of adultery? Where does the root of the sin develop?

Matthew 5:27–30 _____

Matthew 15:19 _____

2. When the teachers and the Pharisees brought to Jesus a woman who had been caught in adultery, what did Jesus say to her accusers?

John 8:3–7 _____

_____

3. After the accusers left, what did Jesus say to the woman?

John 8:8–11 _____

_____

4. How does the Apostle Paul set apart sexual immorality from other sins?

1 Corinthians 6:12–20 _____

_____

5. What are two practical steps that Joseph took to avoid committing adultery with Potiphar's wife?

Genesis 39:10, 12 _____

_____

6. After David committed adultery with Bathsheba, he cried out to God. In Psalm 51, look at the verbs in his prayer. List up to 10 things that David specifically asked of God.

Psalm 51 _____

_____

_____

INTERPRET

1. God uses the metaphor of adultery to describe "faithless Israel." Why is this imagery an appropriate description? How are Israel's sin and the sin of adultery similar?

Jeremiah 3:1–9 _____

APPLY

Read the following Scriptures. Then list the steps that you can take to guard yourself against sexual immorality.

Proverbs 4:23, 25 _____

Matthew 5:27–28 _____

1 Corinthians 15:33 _____

If you have committed adultery, read the passages below and list several truths that God gives you to hold on to.

Psalm 51:17 _____

Psalm 103:8–13 _____

1 Timothy 1:15–16_____

Have you been hurt by the sin of adultery or other sinful actions? What promises does God offer to you? Thank God for these promises and cling to them.

Psalm 3:3–5 _____

Isaiah 26:3 _____

Lamentations 3:19–25 _____

THE EIGHTH COMMANDMENT: EXODUS 20:15

YOU SHALL NOT STEAL.

ARE WE THIEVES?

:: BY PAUL BLACKHAM

It's amazing how theft can irritate us. If someone takes something that belongs to us, even if it is a very small thing, we find it difficult to forget. Even if we pretend that everything is OK, so often the theft is remembered years after it happened. Why is this? Is it that stealing is so wrong? Or is it that we value our possessions so much?

Jesus did not give His interpretation of the Eighth Commandment when He delivered the Sermon on the Mount, but it may be worthwhile for us to contemplate what He might have said about it. If we are guilty of having committed adultery as soon as we lust, if we are guilty of murder as soon as we wish ill of someone, then what attitudes or thoughts show that we are as thieves?

It is tempting to think that covetousness is the attitude or thought that makes us out to be thieves, but *"you shall not covet"*[1] is a Commandment all by itself. Rather, I believe that we are thieves when we wish to improve ourselves at the expense of someone else. Perhaps we do not covet what they have, but we want to advance our own property or status at someone else's cost.

Matthew Henry, a Bible expositor and commentator, wrote that the Eighth Commandment forbids us to "rob others by removing the ancient landmarks, invading our neighbor's rights, taking his goods from his person, or house, or field, forcibly or clandestinely, overreaching in bargains, not restoring what is borrowed or found, withholding just debts or rents or wages."[2]

Although theologian Friedrich Schleiermacher was not an evangelical Christian, he preached a sermon in the early 19th century that showed an awareness of the far-reaching nature of the Eighth Commandment. Schleiermacher said, "Before you think of being benevolent and supporting the needy, be just, set aside all injustice, however secret. ... A society from which all injustice of this kind is not banished is not honored but shamed by even the most generous philanthropy."[3] A generous gift of "stolen" money is not a godly gift.

THE TEN COMMANDMENTS

Obeying the Ten Commandments is deeper than simply not walking out of shops without paying for goods. We can be "stealing" in much more subtle ways. God is asking not only for outward, formal obedience but also for a thorough, heartfelt conformity to His mind and heart.

The Ten Commandments are not just free-floating moral principles; they are the summary statement of all the Laws that the Lord God gave to His people after He redeemed them out of Egypt. The Ten Commandments are addressed to *"the church in the wilderness."*[4]

These Laws are a manifesto for Gospel living—that is to say, the Law did not describe the way a person could become redeemed. Rather, the Law described how God's redeemed people should behave after they have been redeemed. The Ten Commandments begin with the phrase, *"I am the Lord your God who [redeemed] you out of Egypt."*[5] The Law was given to those who already trusted in God.

This is why these Laws have nothing to do with self-righteous, self-satisfied morality. In the Torah we see that there is profound care for the socially disadvantaged, especially for the widow and the orphan. The Lord God Himself cares for those who have no one else to care for them, and we are to do likewise.

LIVING OUT THE EIGHTH COMMANDMENT

Soon after the Ten Commandments are given, God explains them in more detail, beginning with Exodus 20:22.

God doesn't work through the Commandments from One to Ten; He treats them as a package. In Exodus 22 God deals with social justice issues that relate to the Eighth Commandment: *"Do not mistreat an alien or oppress him, for you were aliens in Egypt. Do not take advantage of a widow or an orphan. If you do and they cry out to me, I will certainly hear their cry. My anger will be aroused, and I will kill you with the sword; your wives will become widows and your children fatherless. If you lend money to one of my people among you who is needy, do not be like a moneylender; charge him no interest."*[6]

It is not enough for us to refrain from shoplifting—no, we are to live out the Eighth Commandment in a positive way. Because some of the Ten Commandments are set in the form of "you shall not," we may have a tendency to think that so long as we avoid those specific activities, we have obeyed the Commandments. However, bound up with each "you shall not" is the alternative "you shall": *"You shall not steal,"*[7] and, "You shall care for others."

We are not to live at the expense of another. We are not to take advantage of any person, even if it costs us money and convenience.

The Egyptians had prospered at the expense of the Israelites. They had forced labor from them, treating the Israelites the most harshly when they were the most needy. The Israelites were to remember this whenever they themselves had the upper hand over people in need.

TREASURE IN HEAVEN

The Israelites' day-to-day commercial life was not to have the hard-bitten character of the unmerciful business world. The Israelites were to be deliberate about leaving produce for the hungry: *"When you reap the harvest of your land, do not reap to the very edges of your field or gather the gleanings of your harvest. Do not go over your vineyard a second time or pick up the grapes that have fallen. Leave them for the poor and the alien. I am the Lord your God. Do not steal."*[8]

The context of this passage helps us to see that if we earn our money in such a way that the poor and "the foreigner" suffer, then we have broken the Eighth Commandment.

We need to think carefully about our economic activities in light of this Commandment. Not many of us try to take goods out of a store without paying for them, but it may well be that people are being exploited to produce the goods that we buy. Do we know which companies have ethical policies and which do not? We steal when we buy items that have been produced unfairly. The Eighth Commandment forces us to take these matters seriously.

BEING AN ASSET TO OTHERS

The Apostle Paul, in the New Testament, sheds light on this Commandment: *"He who has been stealing must steal no longer, but must work, doing something useful with his own hands, that he may have something to share with those in need."*[9]

A thief must stop thieving—that is, he must do something useful and share with others. Until the thief does something useful, he hasn't really fulfilled the admonition.

Although the converted thief needs to give special thought to reforming his or her unproductive lifestyle, it is wrong for *anyone*, whatever his or her sins, to behave as a thief behaves. Rather than being an unnecessary burden to others, we are to be an asset to others. This principle shouldn't be restricted simply to economic employment but should be expanded to cover all aspects of life.

Whether we work for money or serve in other ways, we cannot be self-serving. In our homes and families, in our local church, in our workplace, in our school—we must be those who have something to share: *"In everything I did, I showed you that by this kind of hard work we must help the weak, remembering the words the Lord Jesus himself said: 'It is more blessed to give than to receive.'"*[10]

SPIRIT OF GENEROSITY

The book of Acts shows us what Christianity looks like in practice. Acts 2:44–47 has always been a source of challenge to the Church. I don't believe that we have to live in a commune, but the same spirit of extravagant generosity that was present in the Early Church must be our hallmark. Everything that we possess is freely given to us by God, so we are not to hold on to anything as if it were our right.[11]

God reminded the Israelites of this same principle: *"You may say to yourself, 'My power and the strength of my hands have produced this wealth for me.' But remember the Lord your God, for it is he who gives you the ability to produce wealth."*[12]

We are stewards, putting God's generous provision to Gospel use. We are not our own, but we have been bought with the blood of God.[13] We are not to view ourselves as self-sufficient or self-made people. We are under orders, we are "slaves to righteousness"[14]—and it is this that helps us to keep our rights and possessions in perspective. It is not what we have that matters; it is what we do with what we have. It is only as we live out this truth that we fulfill the Eighth Commandment.

---

(1) Exodus 20:17, NIV. (2) From "Exodus," in *Commentary on the Whole Bible,* by Matthew Henry, ©1960 Marshall, Morgan & Scott, Ltd., London, England; ©1961 Zondervan Publishing House, a division of Baker Book House Company, Grand Rapids, Michigan. (3) From "Christian Philanthropy," by Friedrich Schleiermacher, quoted by Karl Barth, in *The Theology of Schleiermacher,* ©1982 Wm. B. Eerdmans Publishing Company, Grand Rapids, Michigan; translated from the Swiss edition of *Karl Barth: Die Theologie Schleiermachers,* Vol. 2 of *Karl Barth Gesamtausgabe,* ©1978 Theologischer Verlag Zurich, Zurich, Switzerland. (4) Acts 7:38, KJV. (5) Exodus 20:2, NIV. (6) Exodus 22:21–25, NIV. (7) Exodus 20:15, NIV. (8) Leviticus 19:9–11, NIV. (9) Ephesians 4:28, NIV. (10) Acts 20:35, NIV. (11) 1 Chronicles 29:10–12. (12) Deuteronomy 8:17–18, NIV. (13) Acts 20:28. (14) Romans 6:18, NIV.

Paul Blackham, Ph.D., is the curate of All Souls Church (Church of England), Langham Place, in London, England. He and his wife, Elizabeth, are parents of two sons and live in London. ©2000 Billy Graham Evangelistic Association.

WHEN DO WE STEAL?

:: BY JAMES M. BOICE

The view that one should not steal is a generally accepted standard of the human race, but only biblical religion shows why stealing is wrong. What the other person rightly possesses has been imparted to him or her by God: *"Every good endowment and every perfect gift is from above, coming down from the Father."*[1] Therefore, to steal from another person is to sin against God.

Of course, theft is also an offense against others. Theft always diminishes them, for it treats them as being unworthy of our respect or love. Even in this, we sin against God, since it is He who has given value to the other person.

We are not to think that we have kept this Commandment just because we have not broken into a home and walked off with someone else's possessions.

There are different subjects from whom we can steal: God, others or ourselves. There are many ways to steal: by stealth, violence or deceit. There are many objects that we can steal: money, time or a person's reputation.

We steal from God when we fail to worship as we ought or when we set our own concerns ahead of His. We steal from Him when we spend our time in personal self-indulgence and do not tell others of God's grace.

We steal from an employer when we do not give the best work of which we are capable or when we overextend our coffee breaks or leave work early. We steal when we waste the raw materials with which we are working. We steal when, as merchants, we charge too much for our products. We steal when we sell inferior products, pretending that they are better than they are.

We steal from our employees when their work environment harms their health or when we do not pay them enough to guarantee healthy, adequate living. We steal by mismanaging others' money. We steal when we borrow but do not repay loans on time or at all. We steal from ourselves when we waste our resources, whether time, talents or money. We steal when we indulge ourselves in material goods while others go without the necessities of existence: food, clothing, shelter or medical care.

The positive side of this Commandment is obvious: We are to do everything in our power to prosper others, helping them to attain their full potential. The Lord God captures this duty in the Golden Rule: *"Whatever you wish that men would do to you, do so to them; for this is the law and the prophets."*[2]

---

(1) James 1:17, RSV. (2) Matthew 7:12, RSV.

James M. Boice, D.Theol. (1938–2000), was senior pastor at Tenth Presbyterian Church (Presbyterian Church in America), in Philadelphia, Pennsylvania. A prolific writer, he was the author of more than 60 books. He and his wife, Linda, parents of three daughters, made their home in Philadelphia. This work is taken by permission from *Foundations of the Christian Faith: A Comprehensive and Readable Theology*, by James Montgomery Boice, ©1986 InterVarsity Christian Fellowship/USA; InterVarsity Press, Downers Grove, Illinois; Inter-Varsity Press—U.K., Leicester, England.

FOUNDATIONS FOR LIFE
:: A CLOSER LOOK ::

The Eighth Commandment: *"You shall not steal"* (Exodus 20:15, NKJV).

OBSERVE

1. In the New Testament, what does Jesus say is the source or motivation for stealing?

Matthew 15:18–20 _____

_____

_____

2. Who is the rightful owner of all things?

Genesis 14:19 _____

_____

Exodus 19:5 _____

_____

Psalm 24:1–2 _____

_____

3. What is one way that a person can steal from God?

Malachi 3:8–10_____

_____

4. What does the Apostle Paul say about thieves and their future inheritance? If a thief turns to Jesus Christ, what hope then does the thief have?

1 Corinthians 6:9–11 _____

_____

_____

Interpret

1. Read Ephesians 4:17–28 where the Apostle Paul writes about how people should live. Is it enough for someone just to quit stealing? Why, or why not?

Ephesians 4:28 _____

_____

_____

_____

_____

2. Explain why stealing may involve more than taking someone else's possessions.

Leviticus 19:9–13 _____

_____

_____

_____

_____

Apply

Read Romans 2:21. Have you been stealing without even realizing it? Think about things you have done that you didn't consider to be stealing, and write down specific ways to avoid breaking this Commandment._____

_____

_____

_____

_____

_____

_____

THE NINTH COMMANDMENT: EXODUS 20:16

YOU SHALL NOT BEAR FALSE WITNESS.

A CALL TO HONESTY

:: *BY JOE M. SPRINKLE*

In August of 1983 I was in Jerusalem. For two exhilarating months I had hiked around the land of the Bible. And in full view of the Temple Mount, where the Dome of the Rock stands, I had studied a bit of modern Hebrew at the Mount Scopus campus of the Hebrew University of Jerusalem, in Israel.

One day I was scheduled to check out of my dorm room by noon. However, I wanted to do a bit of touring that morning, and I did not want to drag around my heavy bags. So, being young and naïve, I put my luggage into the closet and locked the room door. I took off early in the morning, hoping to return by noon.

But I returned late—several hours late, actually. I unlocked the door of my dorm room so that I could grab my stuff and go, but my luggage was gone! I found the woman who had cleaned my room and asked her where she had stored my things. But rather than respond, she looked nervous and did not want to talk to me. So I went to the dorm official who called the woman into his office. "There was no luggage left in that room," she said. I was stunned. She lied!

I never saw my luggage again.

Why do people lie? To protect themselves or others. To hide embarrassing or incriminating acts. To hurt or take advantage of others. But the Ninth Commandment shows God to be the Champion of truth.

THE NINTH COMMANDMENT

The Ninth Commandment has both narrow and broad applications. I translate the Hebrew of that Commandment as follows: "You are not to answer against your neighbor a testimony of a lie."[1] In Hebrew, "answer" (*ʿānāh*) ordinarily refers to a response to a question. A court setting was where an Israelite was most likely to lie in response to questions concerning a neighbor. So the narrow and most concrete application of the Ninth Commandment appears to be the court setting.

Just courts are foundational to an equitable society. In the Mosaic Law witnesses of crimes were required to come forth and testify, and failure to do so was an offense against God that required a sin offering.[2]

To avoid condemning the innocent, God established the rule in Israel that no one could be condemned for a crime on the basis of a single witness; instead, no fewer than two or three witnesses were required.[3] Witnesses in court were charged to be scrupulously honest: not spreading slander or mere rumors[4]; not being swayed by others, no matter how important or numerous they may be[5]; not allowing pity for the accused to distort one's testimony[6]; not accepting any bribes from the parties involved[7]; and not showing prejudice against one who is an outsider.[8]

To deter perjury a witness who testified falsely could be punished with the same penalty that the court would have inflicted on the one that he or she had falsely accused.[9] Hence, if someone falsely accused another of a capital offense, that false witness was subject to execution—*"life for life."*[10]

Courts today fall short of this ideal. Professor Alan M. Dershowitz, at Harvard Law School, in Cambridge, Massachusetts, stated, "On the basis of my academic and professional experience, I believe that no felony is committed more frequently in this country than the genre of perjury and false statements."[11]

A recent survey of more than 50 U.S. state and federal judges, as well as lawyers and academics, conducted by the *ABA Journal*, found that most of the judges interviewed said that increasingly "lawyers appearing before them are bending the truth, not telling the whole truth or just plain lying."[12]

It appears that the American justice system has much to learn from the seriousness with which biblical Law treated perjury!

APPLICATION OF THE NINTH COMMANDMENT

However, the Ninth Commandment's application need not be limited to perjury. The Mosaic Law already finds broader application for this Commandment by condemning lies generally.[13] Moreover, this Commandment, in principle, also condemns such things as deception, gossip, slander and treachery.

Behind the prohibition against false testimony is a positive principle affirming truth. Unlike us, God is true and does not lie[14]; indeed, He cannot lie.[15] Moreover, God wants the righteous to put aside falsehood and speak truth from the heart,[16] expressing love by rejoicing in the truth rather than evil.[17]

Lies are part of the old, pre-Christian self that the believer has put off.[18] Lying is unbecoming of anyone indwelt by the *"Spirit of truth."*[19]

But the devil is a liar in whom there is no truth.[20] The serpent in the garden of Eden told the Bible's first lie to entice Eve to eat the forbidden fruit.[21] Similarly, the wicked are characterized by lies[22]; and they, like the devil, will have no part in the New Jerusalem, but instead be doomed to the lake of fire.[23]

Jesus and the Gospel message are both labeled *"the truth,"*[24] and it is grave indeed when people tell lies in God's name, or reject or distort the truth of the Gospel.[25] The book of Revelation portrays a figure labeled *"the false prophet"*[26] as being cast into the lake of fire.[27] By such passages the Bible in effect asserts, "Woe to those so-called ministers whose false testimony perverts Gospel truth!"

HOW STRICTLY ARE WE TO APPLY THE NINTH COMMANDMENT?

It is clear, then, that the Ninth Commandment discourages lying, but how strictly are we to apply it? Does the Commandment condemn every lie or deception? Does it condemn deceptive tactics in war as when Gideon, by smashing jars and blowing trumpets, caused the Midianites to think that his army was much larger than a mere 300 men?[28] If so, why does Scripture not make a condemnatory aside for this act?

Does the Ninth Commandment prohibit undercover police "sting" operations in which police pretend to be criminals in order to gather evidence for the good cause of punishing the wicked? And what about cases of lies designed to avoid greater evils, such as when Rahab the harlot lied to protect the lives of the Israelite spies?[29]

Or is the Ninth Commandment similar to the Sixth Commandment with its prohibition against the taking of human life,[30] a prohibition for which God allowed Israel exceptions (for war and for capital offenses)?

Most Christians tolerate mild, "polite" deceptions where one's response is misleading to avoid unnecessary offense. But once we start justifying a lie for a "greater good," condoning almost any lie or deception can easily follow.

The story of Rahab is an interesting one for Christian ethicists. Some Christians believe that it is only lies intended to harm one's neighbor that are condemned by the Ninth Commandment.

Other Christians believe that Rahab's lie, being for purposes of justice and to thwart evil, was no sin at all but a service of love. Martin Luther wrote, "It is a respectable and pious lie and should rather be called a service of love."[31]

Still other Christians insist that a lie is always wrong; therefore, when we are forced by circumstance or lack of imagination to choose a lie over some more serious evil, after choosing to lie, we should confess our sin for having done so. Though there may be circumstances where a lie may be chosen as the lesser evil, I am reluctant to call such a lie good. In any case, the whole tenor of Scripture suggests that such circumstances are rare.

In our present age where Postmodernism denies that absolute truth exists, the absolute truth of the Gospel needs to be given credibility by Christians proving themselves scrupulously truthful. The Ninth Commandment, though stated negatively as a *"thou shalt not,"*[32] has its positive implication: a call to honesty, candor and integrity.

(1) Cf. Exodus 20:16. (2) Leviticus 5:1, 5–6. (3) Deuteronomy 19:15. (4) Exodus 23:1. (5) Exodus 23:2. (6) Exodus 23:3. (7) Exodus 23:8. (8) Exodus 23:9. (9) Deuteronomy 19:16–19. (10) Deuteronomy 19:21, NIV. (11) From the testimony of Professor Alan M. Dershowitz, Harvard Law School, in Cambridge, Massachusetts, before the U.S. House of Representatives Judiciary Committee, in Washington, D.C., December 1, 1998. (12) From "The Lies Have It," by Mark Curriden, in *ABA Journal*, May 1995, ©1995 *ABA Journal*, Chicago, Illinois. (13) Leviticus 19:11. (14) Numbers 23:19. (15) Hebrews 6:18. (16) Ephesians 4:25. (17) 1 Corinthians 13:6. (18) Colossians 3:9. (19) John 16:13, NIV. (20) John 8:44. (21) Genesis 3:4. (22) Psalm 5:5–6. (23) Revelation 21:27; 22:15. (24) John 14:6, NIV. (25) Jeremiah 14:14; Acts 21:24. (26) Revelation 20:10, NIV. (27) Revelation 20:10. (28) Judges 7:19–21. (29) Joshua 2:3–6. (30) Exodus 20:13. (31) From *Luther's Works: Lectures on Genesis 26–30*, by Martin Luther, Vol. 5, edited by Jaroslav Pelikan, ©1968 Concordia Publishing House, Concordia Publishing House, St. Louis, Missouri. (32) Exodus 20:16, KJV.

Joe M. Sprinkle, Ph.D., is professor of Old Testament at Crossroads College in Rochester, Minnesota. He and his wife, Christilee, are parents of two daughters. ©2000 Billy Graham Evangelistic Association.

WHY NOT TELL LIES?

:: BY F.B. HUEY JR.

The Command not to bear false witness against one's neighbor[1] originated in the setting of the court where witnesses were under oath to tell the truth. But in its broader application it is a prohibition against untruthfulness of any kind.[2]

A false witness could bring about the death of an innocent person[3] or destroy the reputation of another person.[4] The seriousness of this sin lies in the fact that an attack on another person is an attack against God, and God is jealous for His creation.

The tongue is a powerful weapon[5]; it can destroy as surely as killing does, whether it is a malicious lie, idle gossip, propaganda or a half-truth. Insincere flattery or keeping silent when another person's reputation is being unjustly maligned violates the spirit of this Command.

The New Testament counterpart of the Ninth Commandment is to speak the truth in love.[6]

---

(1) Exodus 20:16. (2) Leviticus 19:11; Hosea 4:2. (3) 1 Kings 21:10, 13; Matthew 26:59–61. (4) Deuteronomy 19:16–19. (5) James 3:5–6. (6) Ephesians 4:15; 4:25; 6:14.

This article is taken by permission from *Exodus: A Study Guide Commentary*, by F.B. Huey Jr., ©1977 The Zondervan Corporation, Zondervan Publishing House, Grand Rapids, Michigan.

FOUNDATIONS FOR LIFE
:: A CLOSER LOOK ::

The Ninth Commandment: *"You shall not bear false witness against your neighbor"* (Exodus 20:16, NKJV).

OBSERVE

1. What was the penalty for perjury in biblical law?
Deuteronomy 19:15–21 _____

_____

2. What will be the destiny of those who practice lies?
Revelation 21:8_____

_____

3. Why should believers not lie, according to the Apostle Paul?
Colossians 3:8–10 _____

_____

INTERPRET

1. In John 8:42–47 Jesus is speaking about unbelief and the *"father of lies"* (John 8:44, RSV). What connection does Jesus draw between the two? _____

_____

_____

2. Read Psalm 12. In what specific ways does our culture reflect the conditions listed in this Psalm?_____

_____

_____

3. Ephesians 4:25 tells Christians not to lie but to speak truthfully to each other. Ephesians 4:15 tells us to speak the truth in love. Are there circumstances when speaking the truth may be wrong or unloving? Explain. _____

_____

_____

_____

_____

APPLY

Have you ever wronged someone by lies or deception? If so, ask God for forgiveness, and if possible ask forgiveness from the person or people that you hurt. Pray that God would make you a person of honesty and integrity.

_____

_____

_____

_____

_____

_____

_____

THE TENTH COMMANDMENT: EXODUS 20:17

YOU SHALL NOT COVET.

COVETOUSNESS— WANTING WHAT WE DON'T HAVE

:: *BY J. ROBERT VANNOY*

We had just moved into a small house, with our four young children, in a village about 30 minutes outside Amsterdam, The Netherlands. I was to spend the year at the Free University of Amsterdam working on my doctoral dissertation. Our children had left behind their friends and the security of the only home that they had ever known to settle into village life in a foreign country. All of this was without the companionship of our trusted dog, a chocolate lab named Tobler, which we had left with friends in the United States.

One day there was a knock on the door—our oldest son, six years of age, had been brought home to his mother by the keeper of a small park about a block from our house. A section of this park, surrounded by a high fence, contained some animals including rabbits, ducks and a few deer. According to the park custodian, our son had climbed the fence, captured a rabbit and was on his way back over the fence with the rabbit under his arm when he was apprehended.

My wife explained to the keeper that we had just arrived in the village, and that our son had been forced to leave his cherished dog back in the United States, and that this was probably the explanation for his inappropriate behavior.

While this story is an example of a small child's way of dealing with feeling lonesome and discontent by first desiring, and then taking, something that did not belong to him, it uncovers the proclivity that lies deep within all of us to desire things that we have no right to have.

THE GENERAL REQUIREMENTS OF THE
TENTH COMMANDMENT

The Tenth Commandment[1] addresses an inner attitude rather than an outward act. The Westminster Shorter Catechism rightly identifies "full contentment with our own condition, with a right and charitable frame of spirit toward our neighbor, and all that is his"[2] as that which this Commandment requires.

Further, in the Westminster Shorter Catechism, the Tenth Commandment accordingly forbids "all discontentment with our own estate, envying or grieving at the good of our neighbor, and all inordinate motions and affections to any thing that is his."[2] Because covetousness expresses dissatisfaction with God's providential ordering of our lives, covetousness is an issue of the heart. Jesus said that out of the heart come *"evil thoughts, murder, adultery, all other sexual immorality, theft, lying, and slander."*[3]

THE SPECIFIC FOCUS OF THE
TENTH COMMANDMENT

Scholars have debated where to place the specific focus of the Tenth Commandment.[4] Although interpreters agree that covetousness is an illicit desire, it is possible to distinguish between four stages of such a desire.

We all have had the experience of an improper desire springing up in our heart. This may be termed the first stage.

When this happens, it is possible to cultivate that desire or to seek immediately God's grace to banish it from our hearts and minds. This action is the second stage.

Should we, however, nourish the desire and submit to its power, we may begin to devise a plan to satisfy that illicit desire. This is the third stage.

When that plan has been conceived, if there is still no inner cleansing of the heart and mind by a work of God's grace, then a sinful act that breaks one of the previously given nine Commandments may be performed. This fourth stage is the sins specifically addressed in the Commandments prohibiting adultery, stealing, murder.

So the question concerning the precise focus of the Tenth Commandment is, Which of the four stages of illicit desire does the Tenth Commandment address?

Some scholars have suggested that the Tenth Commandment addresses only the first two of these stages: the conceiving and nurturing of an illicit desire. Other scholars view the third stage not only as something that is included in the intent of the Tenth Commandment but in fact is its most important part. According to this understanding, it is the strategizing on how to get whatever we desire that is the central focus of the Tenth Commandment.

To complicate further the picture, some have suggested that we are not culpable for spontaneous illicit desires if we do not nurture or fulfill them. How can we help it if some improper desire arises within us? If we do not cultivate the desire, then it is said that it is nothing for which we will be held accountable by God. Those of this persuasion would say that only stages two and three are included in the purview of the Tenth Commandment.

The Apostle James wrote that *"temptation comes from the lure of our own evil desires. These evil desires lead to evil actions, and evil actions lead to death."*[5] The Greek word for "desire" in James' statement (*epithumia*) is the same word (in its noun form) that is used to translate the Hebrew verb for "covet" in Exodus 20:17. So the *"evil desires"*[5] of James' statement addresses the same issue that is censured by the Tenth Commandment.

Likewise, according to the Heidelberg Catechism, the Tenth Commandment requires that "there should never enter our heart even the least inclination or thought contrary to any Commandment of God, but that we should always hate sin with our whole heart and find satisfaction and joy in all righteousness."[6]

So with some degree of reflection, we can understand that the seemingly simple statement of Exodus 20:17 prohibiting illicit desires penetrates deeply into the fallen nature of our human heart and ultimately leaves none of us free from the failure to live up to its requirements.

It would seem, then, that the Tenth Commandment addresses all three stages in the progression of illicit desire that lead up to the committing of evil acts. So here is a clear warning that we are not to nourish illicit desires, nor are we to devise strategies for achieving what those desires demand.

THE BROADER IMPLICATIONS OF THE TENTH COMMANDMENT

In our time and culture the radical nature of the Tenth Commandment is particularly appropriate. Western society not only encourages discontentment with the station in life where God has placed us but also fosters inordinate desires for self-gratification of all kinds. Envy and greed have become major forces in the consumption-driven capitalism of modern Western culture. It is extremely difficult to avoid being swept along in the currents of the hundreds of deceptively attractive appeals to the self-centered desires of the human heart that we encounter each day of our lives.

The Bible is clear in its assessment of these things. Jesus said, *"Take heed, and beware of covetousness: for a man's life consisteth not in the abundance of the things which he possesseth."*[7] The author of Hebrews wrote, *"Stay away from the love of money; be satisfied with what you have."*[8] To the Colossians the Apostle Paul wrote, *"Covetousness ... is idolatry,"*[9] and to Timothy Paul wrote, *"True religion with contentment is great wealth."*[10]

Paul went on, *"So if we have enough food and clothing, let us be content. But people who long to be rich fall into temptation and are trapped by many foolish and harmful desires that plunge them into ruin and destruction. For the love of money is at the root of all kinds of evil. And some people, craving money, have wandered from the faith and pierced themselves with many sorrows."*[11] How urgently these words need to be heard again and taken seriously by Christians.

AN ISSUE OF THE HEART

At its root the sin of covetousness is an issue of the heart. It is something that cannot be controlled by symptomatic treatment. Suppression of its powerful influence in our daily lives requires the transforming power of an inner life wholly committed to an obedient and faithful following of Christ.

Paul put the fundamental issue in stark terms when he wrote, *"I have been crucified with Christ and I no longer live, but Christ lives in me. The life I live in the body, I live by faith in the Son of God, who loved me and gave himself for me."* [12]

It is nothing short of this daily dying to self and living to serve Christ that will break the shackles of the universal human inclination to make idols out of personal possessions. We need the grace to say with Paul, *"Oh, what a miserable person I am! Who will free me from this life that is dominated by sin? Thank God! The answer is in Jesus Christ our Lord."* [13]

---

(1) Exodus 20:17. (2) From the *Westminster Confession of Faith: The Shorter Catechism*, Free Presbyterian Publications, Glasgow, Scotland, 1966, 1973. (3) Matthew 15:19, NLT. (4) In *The Ten Commandments: Manual for the Christian Life*, by J. Douma, translated by Nelson D. Kloosterman, English translation ©1966 Nelson D. Kloosterman, P&R Publishing Company, Phillipsburg, New Jersey (originally published as *De Tien Geboden: Handreiking voor het Christelijk*, by Uitgeverij Van den Berg, Kampen, 1992). (5) James 1:14–15, NLT. (6) From *The Heidelberg Catechism With Commentary*, ©1962, 1963 United Church Press, Philadelphia, Pennsylvania. (7) Luke 12:15, KJV. (8) Hebrews 13:5, NLT. (9) Colossians 3:5, KJV. (10) 1 Timothy 6:6, NLT. (11) 1 Timothy 6:8–10, NLT. (12) Galatians 2:20, NIV. (13) Romans 7:24–25, NLT.

J. Robert Vannoy is a former professor of Old Testament and one of the founders of Biblical Theological Seminary in Hatfield, Pennsylvania. He and his wife, Kathe, are parents of four grown children and live in Souderton. ©2000 Billy Graham Evangelistic Association.

THE DANGER OF DISSATISFACTION

:: BY PETER HOLWERDA

To covet is to desire earnestly or long for something or someone. We all covet to a certain extent. It is natural and necessary for us to do so as human beings. There are legitimate things to covet. We do well if we cry with the psalmist, *"As the hart panteth after the water brooks, so panteth my soul after thee, O God"* (Psalm 42:1, KJV).

The terrible fact, however, is that human nature has been perverted through sin, and the proper desires have been drawn away from their proper objects and twisted out of shape. We need to recognize that our desires may be stimulated or restrained, multiplied, corrected or perverted.

God has ordained a proper way to the obtaining of a spouse and possessions. The danger in many cases is that we are not satisfied with this arrangement, and we tend by selfish longings and envious eyes to cross the boundaries that He has established.

To covet in this way is to be dissatisfied with the provisions that God has made. It is to violate the Commandment to love one's neighbor as oneself. It is refusing to be ruled by Him in our hearts, and it is elevating self to the throne. This is called idolatry. The individual in such a state is in a dangerous way, for a covetous person cannot enter the Kingdom of heaven. God abhors a covetous person. Truly we should pray to be kept and delivered from such a state.

This article is taken by permission from "The Tenth Commandment," by Peter Holwerda, in *Sermons on the Ten Commandments*, edited by Henry H. Kuiper, ©1951 Zondervan Publishing House, Grand Rapids, Michigan.

FOUNDATIONS FOR LIFE
:: A CLOSER LOOK ::

The Tenth Commandment: *"You shall not covet your neighbor's house; you shall not covet your neighbor's wife, nor his male servant, nor his female servant, nor his ox, nor his donkey, nor anything that is your neighbor's"* (Exodus 20:17, NKJV).

OBSERVE

1. What message does Jesus give about covetousness (or greed)?
Luke 12:13–15 _____

_____

_____

_____

2. What should be our motivation to be contented?
Hebrews 13:5 _____

_____

_____

_____

_____

_____

_____

3. What does the Apostle Paul say is the result of pursuing money or of not being contented?
1 Timothy 6:6–10 _____

_____

_____

_____

INTERPRET

1. Read Colossians 3:5. Paul calls covetousness "idolatry."
   What is the relationship between covetousness and idolatry?

   _____

   _____

   _____

2. Why will someone who loves wealth never be satisfied?
   Ecclesiastes 5:10–14 _____

   _____

   _____

   _____

   _____

APPLY

What are some ways that covetousness manifests itself in your
life? _____

   _____

   _____

   _____

   _____

   _____

Pray that God will give you a contented heart.

THE GREATEST COMMANDMENT

LOVE THE LORD YOUR GOD WITH ALL YOUR HEART AND WITH ALL YOUR SOUL AND WITH ALL YOUR MIND. LOVE YOUR NEIGHBOR AS YOURSELF.

THE VERY HEART OF THE MATTER

:: *BY VERN SHERIDAN POYTHRESS*

The Ten Commandments represent God's own summary of our duties toward Him. How valuable to have God lay out His instructions in a space of only 17 verses. But how difficult it is to obey them!

STRUGGLES AND QUESTIONS

One month, while I was in college, I struggled with what it meant to obey God and to follow Him. I went from one extreme to another.

For a while I devoted myself fanatically to obeying God's Commandments. But I became stiff and artificial in my obedience. I was miserable. I came to my senses only when a fellow Christian reminded me of God's love. God's grace to me did not depend on my scrupulosity, but on His forgiveness and on His having accepted me through Jesus Christ. How could I have forgotten such a basic truth?

So I went to the other extreme. Feeling free because of God's love, I decided to do what I wanted, regardless of what anyone thought. But then another fellow Christian gently pointed out to me that I was hurting other people by my lack of consideration for them.

I had to take stock. Neither way had worked. Neither way had honored God. So what was the answer? I did not know. I decided that I had to follow Christ and have personal communion with Him, without having a regimental formula.

THE GREATEST COMMANDMENT

If I had thought about it, I could have received decisive guidance from a passage in the Gospel of Matthew where Jesus indicates how to serve God. One of the Pharisees tested Jesus with a question, *"Teacher, which is the greatest commandment in the Law?"*[1]

Jesus answered, *"'Love the Lord your God with all your heart and with all your soul and with all your mind.' This is the first and greatest commandment. And the second is like it: 'Love your neighbor as yourself.' All the Law and the Prophets hang on these two commandments."*[2]

LOVING GOD

The Pharisees prided themselves on meticulous observance of the Law. They knew the Ten Commandments, but they paid rigorous attention to all the laws in the books of Moses—613 laws,[3] according to a traditional count. They tried to reason out the implications of the laws, and to make sure that they avoided even the possibility of violating any of them.

But the Pharisees had lost sight of the very heart of the matter—loving God. Without love for God, the external observance of the Commandments becomes empty actions. Jesus warned of this danger: *"Woe to you, teachers of the law and Pharisees, you hypocrites! You clean the outside of the cup and dish, but inside they are full of greed and self-indulgence. Blind Pharisee! First clean the inside of the cup and dish, and then the outside also will be clean."*[4]

Loving God means receiving cleansing inside first. Only in this way is our obedience genuine. Otherwise, even though we may appear to others to be righteous, our obedience is corrupted by bad motives.

God Himself gave us the central Commandment to love God, along with the other Commandments.[5] This central command helps to define the spirit in which we must keep all the Commandments. If we are not ardently following this one command, we are not keeping any of the others either.

The example of the Pharisees shows that when we fail to be in personal communion with God and to love Him fervently, we also are apt to misinterpret the Bible, as the Sadducees did. Jesus bluntly told the Sadducees, *"You are wrong, because you know neither the scriptures nor the power of God."*[6] Jesus criticized the Pharisees and the scribes because they transgressed the Commandment of God for the sake of their traditions.[7]

FULL DEVOTION

What then did Jesus say? *"Love the Lord your God with all your heart and with all your soul and with all your mind."*[8] Heart and soul and mind are not three distinct pieces of ourselves that we may offer to God. They all point to what we really are. The Bible indicates that our heart is central: *"The good man brings good things out of the good stored up in his heart, and the evil man brings evil things out of the evil stored up in his heart. For out of the overflow of his heart his mouth speaks."*[9] Everything we are and have, beginning with our inmost commitments and all our thoughts, we must devote to loving, adoring and serving God.

THE HEARTBEAT OF ALL THE COMMANDMENTS

Jesus then said, that *"[to love God] is the first and greatest commandment."*[10] It is first and greatest in that it represents the heartbeat of all the Commandments.

Note that it is the first Commandment, but not the only one. Jesus said, *"If you love me, you will keep my commandments."*[11] That is, if we truly love God, we will keep all the other Commandments as well as this, the greatest one.

Today we need this reminder to obey all the Commandments of God. Some people believe that "love" is merely a happy feeling of friendliness or good will. They think that if they feel good about the idea of God, then they may do as they please. Indeed, an approach called "situation ethics" claimed that love *replaced* all the Commandments. But that is not a biblical conception of loving God. Love does not replace Commandments. Love gives us the right motive so that we genuinely can obey the Commandments.

This is true even on a human level. What would a mother think if her eight-year-old boy continually says that he loves her, but then he disobeys, talks back to her, and never helps out? In First John we read, *"Let us not love with words or tongue but with actions and in truth."*[12]

Really loving God means honoring Him, revering Him and paying close attention to His desires as expressed in the Bible. And not only are we to pay attention, but we are to obey. The Bible warns, *"Do not merely listen to the word, and so deceive yourselves. Do what it says."*[13]

THE RIGHT WAY

What wise direction Jesus gives! He shows us how to avoid both the errors that I fell into in college.

On the one side, Jesus directs us beyond legalism by starting with the central issue of our communion with God. Are we devoted to God, or are we devoted to ourselves? Have we asked God to clean our hearts?

On the other side, Jesus leads us beyond an irresponsible idea of freedom by indicating that God expects us to obey Him and not just have good feelings or wishes. We are to please God by following the ways that He has revealed, not by making up our own ways and calling them religious.

LOVING YOUR NEIGHBOR

Jesus added something more to the greatest Commandment: *"The second is like it: 'Love your neighbor as yourself.'"*[14] In First John the connection is explicit: *"We love because he first loved us. If anyone says, 'I love God,' yet hates his brother, he is a liar. For anyone who does not love his brother, whom he has seen, cannot love God, whom he has not seen. And he has given us this command: Whoever loves God must also love his brother."*[15]

Loving God empowers us to love other people. The Commandments not to murder[16] and not to steal[17] are not just about refraining from evil. When seen in the light of the fundamental principle of loving others, the Commandments imply that we should look for positive ways to enhance the life and prosperity of our neighbors. The focus on love helps us not to settle for a minimum concern for neighbors but to reach out to them. Love helps us to understand the real thrust of the Commandments, and to give us concern for actual obeying, not merely listening.[18]

MEASURING UP TO THE STANDARD

When we read the Sermon on the Mount,[19] we begin to see the deep implications of God's Commandments, and we need to ask ourselves, "Who can do all this? How can I measure up to a standard that asks for perfect motivations as well as full outward obedience?"

You and I do not measure up. But there is One who does. We read in First John, "*In this is love, not that we loved God, but that He loved us and sent His Son to be the propitiation for our sins.*"[20]

Jesus loved us perfectly and gave Himself for us.[21] He saved us because we cannot save ourselves.[22] And now, when we put our trust in Him, we are united to Him, and we are transformed so that we can imitate the pattern of His love: "*A new commandment I give to you, that you love one another; even as I have loved you, that you also love one another. By this all [people] will know that you are my disciples, if you have love for one another.*"[23] Through Jesus Christ we receive not only the understanding of God's will but also the power and the motivation to serve Him. In receiving His love, we can, in turn, love others.

---

(1) Matthew 22:36, NIV. (2) Matthew 22:37–40, NIV. (3) See *New Testament Commentary: Matthew*, by William Hendriksen, Baker Book House Company, Grand Rapids, Michigan. (4) Matthew 23:25–26, NIV. (5) Deuteronomy 6:1–25. (6) Matthew 22:29, RSV. (7) Matthew 15:3. (8) Matthew 22:37, NIV. (9) Luke 6:45, NIV. (10) Matthew 22:38, NIV. (11) John 14:15, RSV. (12) 1 John 3:18, NIV. (13) James 1:22, NIV. (14) Matthew 22:39, NIV. (15) 1 John 4:19–21, NIV. (16) Exodus 20:13. (17) Exodus 20:15. (18) James 1:22. (19) Matthew 5–7. (20) 1 John 4:10, NASB. (21) Galatians 2:20. (22) Romans 5:6–10. (23) John 13:34–35, RSV.

Vern Sheridan Poythress, Th.D., is professor of New Testament interpretation at Westminster Theological Seminary in Philadelphia, Pennsylvania. He also is the author of six books, including *God-Centered Biblical Interpretation*. He and his wife, Diane, are parents of two children and live in Glenside. ©2000 Billy Graham Evangelistic Association.

WHERE LOVE REIGNS

:: *BY H.A. IRONSIDE*

"Thou shalt love the Lord thy God"[1]—If God is loved supremely, no one will violate anything that He has commanded. This covers particularly the first Table of the Law, which sets forth man's duty to God.

"Thou shalt love thy neighbor as thyself"[2]—This originally came from Leviticus 19:18 and covers all of the second Table, for *"love worketh no ill to his neighbor."*[3]

Where love reigns, all else will be as it should be, for no one who truly loves God and his or her neighbor will intentionally wrong either God or neighbor.[4] All the Law and the prophets hang upon these two Commandments cited by Jesus, for every sin that we commit is either a wrong done to God Himself or to our fellow men. The salvation provided for us is first an atonement to meet all our sins, and second a regeneration to enable us to love God and our neighbor so as to cease from sin.

We have become alienated from God through the Fall. When we are born again by the Word and the Holy Spirit, we receive eternal life. The very nature of this new life is love, and therefore love becomes the controlling principle of the life of the person walking with Christ. Walking not after the flesh but after the Holy Spirit, the righteousness of the Law comes to fulfillment,[5] and we find it as easy to love God and our neighbor as it was easy before to live in selfishness and ill will toward others. A new power dominates us. This is the positive evidence of the new birth in Christ.[6]

---

(1) Deuteronomy 6:5, KJV; Matthew 22:37, KJV. (2) Leviticus 19:18, KJV; Matthew 22:39, KJV. (3) Romans 13:10, KJV. (4) Matthew 7:12. (5) Romans 8:4. (6) 1 John 3:14; 1 John 5:1–2.

H.A. Ironside (1876–1951) traveled over much of the United States, Canada and the British Isles, preaching and teaching. He also was a visiting professor at Dallas Theological Seminary and pastor at The Moody Memorial Church in Chicago, Illinois. He wrote many books, including a set of commentaries on the Bible. This work is taken from *Expository Notes on the Gospel of Matthew*, by H.A. Ironside, ©1948 Loizeaux Brothers, Inc., Neptune, New Jersey.

FOUNDATIONS FOR LIFE
:: A CLOSER LOOK ::

The Greatest Commandment: Jesus said, *"'Love the Lord your God with all your heart and with all your soul and with all your mind.' ... 'Love your neighbor as yourself'"* (Matthew 22:37, 39, NIV).

OBSERVE

1. According to Jesus, what is the proof that we love Him?

John 14:15 _____

_____

John 15:9–17 _____

_____

2. In what way are God's two greatest Commandments linked?

1 John 4:19–21 _____

_____

_____

3. What provision does God make for helping us to obey Him?

John 14:15–26 _____

_____

_____

INTERPRET

1. How does God through the Holy Spirit enable us to keep God's Commandments?

Romans 8:1–17 _____

_____

_____

2. In what ways does the work of Jesus Christ alter our understanding of the Old Testament Commandments?

Colossians 2:13–23_____

_____

_____

3. What kind of "freedom" is the Apostle Paul talking about? What would be a correct use of this freedom? What would be an incorrect use of this freedom?

Galatians 5:13–15_____

_____

_____

4. Who is our "neighbor"?

Luke 10:25–37 _____

_____

_____

APPLY

1. In what ways will you teach others the Commandment to love God with all their heart, soul and strength?

Deuteronomy 6:4–9_____

_____

_____

2. List three ways in which you will love someone *"with actions and in truth"* (1 John 3:18, NIV).

1 John 3:17–18 _____

_____

_____

_____

THE TEN COMMANDMENTS

:: *BY BILLY GRAHAM*

Why did God give the Ten Commandments? Moses had led the Israelites out of Egypt, across the Red Sea, then on to Mount Sinai. It was there—amid thunderings, lightning and smoke—that God called Moses to come up to the top of the mountain. It was there, on holy ground, that God gave Moses the tablets of stone on which He had written the Ten Commandments.

They are called the "law," and almost every law today is based in some way on the Ten Commandments. Our moral laws come from the Ten Commandments, because the Commandments set forth not only the holiness and righteousness of God, but also the requirements and the demands of a holy God.

But when God gave the Ten Commandments, He knew that no one could keep them. There is not a person—except Jesus Christ—who has kept the Ten Commandments. For example, Jesus made this explanation about the Commandment *"Thou shalt not kill."*[1] He said that you have broken that commandment if you have ever had hatred toward another person.

WE SEE OURSELVES

If we cannot keep the Commandments, then why did God give them? The Ten Commandments were given, the Bible says, as a *mirror*. The "law" is a mirror. When I look into the Ten Commandments, I see myself—I see how far short I have come of God's requirements.

God says, "Here are the rules to live by; here is the law; here are my requirements. Here is how I want you to live—not only because I require it, but also for your own good and your own benefit." When we read the Commandments and understand them in the light of the Sermon on the Mount,[2] we see ourselves as lawbreakers.

You are a lawbreaker; I am a lawbreaker. I have broken the

Ten Commandments; therefore, I am a sinner. The Bible teaches that God is a holy God and a righteous God, and it teaches that God is going to judge sin. *"The wages of sin is death."*[3] *"The soul who sins shall die."*[4] There is a sentence of spiritual death on every person who is outside of Christ.

You will not be condemned at the judgment; **you are under condemnation now**—separated from God! That is the reason you may be bearing your own burdens, your own trials. That is the reason you haven't found peace and joy and happiness in life—because you are separated from God.

You are a lawbreaker! I read the Ten Commandments and they tell me that you are guilty.

I read another Commandment, and I say, "I am guilty." I am guilty of breaking the law, and I must pay the debt. I must be separated from God because of my sins.

Then the Bible says that the Ten Commandments become a schoolmaster that drives me to repentance.[5] It becomes an usher. In ancient Rome, the usher was a slave who escorted a boy to school and back, and sat by him when he was at his lessons. The usher had no authority to control, no authority to punish, no authority to instruct, only authority to report on misbehavior.

WHICH WAY?

When I see myself in the light of the holy law of God, when I see myself in the light of the person of Jesus Christ, who was an expression of that law, what can I do? Which way can I turn?

There are many people who say, "Well, I'll pile up a lot of good works during my lifetime; and if my good works outweigh my bad works, I'll get to heaven." The Bible doesn't say that!

The Bible says, *"For by grace you have been saved through faith, and that not of yourselves; it is the gift of God, not of works, lest anyone should boast."*[6] By the works of the law shall no man be saved.[7] You can do good works all your life, but that doesn't save your soul!

On many churches you will see a cross. Why? Because when Jesus Christ died on that first Good Friday, He was dying for a special purpose. He wasn't just killed.

It was the love of God that was outpoured. In some mysterious way God took your sins, your guilt, my sins, my guilt, and laid them on Christ.

He became the great Sin-bearer. He died in our place. He shed His blood for our redemption. Unless you have been to the foot of that Cross and repented of your sins and received the Savior, I do not see how you can gain entrance into the Kingdom of heaven.

GOD IS ALL-KNOWING

Let's just look at the Third Commandment for example. It says, *"Thou shalt not take the name of the Lord thy God in vain."*[8] The names of God reveal His attributes. The Bible indicates that God is an all-knowing God.

The Bible says, *"The eyes of the Lord are in every place, keeping watch on the evil and the good."*[9] Think of it now—God's eyes are in every place. There is nothing that you have ever done but that God saw it!

The Bible indicates that God has a set of books and that He is recording everything that you ever do, or think, and even the motives, thoughts and intents of your heart.

You have tried to hide some things in your life, but God sees them as though the blazing sunlight were upon them. God's eyes are watching every moment from the cradle to the grave. God knows and sees.

The Bible teaches that God is holy: *"Exalt the Lord our God, and worship at His footstool; for He is holy."*[10] The Bible teaches that God is love. *"He that loveth not knoweth not God."*[11] All the way through the Bible we find various names for God which describe the kind of person that He is.

GOD'S NAME IS HALLOWED

God is jealous of His name and reputation; and one of the most grievous sins that can be committed is to injure, bring into disrepute or to blaspheme the name of God. People will go to almost any length to protect their names. You have a good name, and we have laws that protect that name against slander. You like to protect that name. It means something to have a good name.

God's name is holy and hallowed, and God is jealous of His name: *"Thou shalt not take the name of the Lord thy God in vain."* [8]

How do we take the name of God in vain?

First, we take the name of God in vain when we speak lightly or irreverently of His name, or if we use profanity. Deuteronomy 28:58 says, *" … that you may fear this glorious and awesome name, THE LORD YOUR GOD."* [12] Jesus, when speaking of His heavenly Father, said, *"Hallowed be thy name."* [13]

When we mention the name of Queen Elizabeth, we give her the title that she deserves. And when we mention the name of the Lord God, it is never to be used in profanity.

You hear people today who take the name of God in vain by profanity and swearing. I tell you it is such a sin against God that He has put it in His Ten Commandments; and it is the only Commandment that has its own built-in judgment: *"The Lord will not hold him guiltless who takes His name in vain."* [14]

I cannot find in the Scriptures a more grievous sin. We use the name of God lightly a thousand times a day. We joke about God. We do not hold Him in reverence.

In contrast, when the old Jewish rabbis were writing and came to the name of the Lord God, they would leave a blank space because they did not feel worthy even to write that holy name. We do not understand the majesty and the glory of God. We do not understand how hallowed His name is.

DO YOU DEFILE GOD'S TEMPLE?

Second, we take the name of God in vain when we defile our bodies. You and I have been created in the image of God. According to the Scriptures, our bodies are the temple of the Holy Spirit. When you mistreat the body, you profane the temple of God.

Perhaps you point at a person because he or she takes a drink—but how about pushing yourself away from the table a little bit earlier?

Once I looked up every Scripture in the Bible that had to do with gluttony. You would be surprised at how much God talks against gluttony. We are guilty of the sin of gluttony. We defile our bodies.

When you engage in sinful and immoral pleasure, you are taking the name of the Lord in vain by defiling your body. When you commit the sin of adultery, when you commit the immoral sexual sins that are prevalent in our day, you defile your body. You are taking the name of God in vain, and God will not hold you guiltless.

PROMISES ARE IMPORTANT!

Third, we take the name of God in vain when we make vows that we don't keep. You may have taken a marriage vow, and you took it in the name of God; but perhaps you haven't kept it.

It would do you good to read your marriage vows to each other at least once a year, and remember the things which you promised. You took that vow in the name of God. It was a holy contract.

As a man you may have been unfaithful to your wife; as a woman you may have been unfaithful to your husband. It could be that you have not cared for your family as you should. There are vows which you have not kept.

You made a vow at confirmation.

You made a vow at the holy rite of baptism.

You made a vow when you took the bread and the cup of communion.

You made a vow when you stood before the deacons or the elders and the board of your church. You made a vow in the name of God, and you haven't kept it. You promised that unless Providence prohibited, you would be in church faithfully on Sunday.

You promised that you would give a part of your income to the work of the Lord. You promised that you would live for God in your daily relationships—you made that vow in the name of God and then you forgot it.

We don't go to church just because we like the minister or do not like the minister. We go to church to worship God. You made a vow that you would meet God in the church; and whether it's a little building or a cathedral, you can worship God—you go to worship Him!

When you joined the church, that was a holy vow in the sight of God. Perhaps it wasn't holy to you, but it was holy in the sight of God. The Scripture says, *"I will pay You my vows, which my lips have uttered ... when I was in trouble."*[15] Have you paid your vows?

ACCEPT CHRIST AS YOUR SAVIOR

If you have been neglectful of your vows and you have not paid your vows, you can renew your vow to God and give your life to Him. You can say, "Oh God, I am sorry. I acknowledge that I have sinned against You by not keeping my vows. I want to give myself afresh to You." He will receive you and forgive you.

If you have never accepted Christ as your Savior, I ask you to give your life to Him right now. The Bible says, *"The blood of Jesus Christ His Son cleanses us from all sin,"*[16] and, *"Whoever calls upon the name of the Lord shall be saved."*[17]

You may never again be this close to the Kingdom of God. The Bible says, *"He who is often reproved, and hardens his neck, will suddenly be destroyed, and that without remedy."*[18] You have been warned, and the Spirit of God has spoken to your heart.

Right now there is a little voice speaking to you; that is the voice of the Spirit of God. You may never again sense His presence quite as strongly as you do right now. This is the moment and this is the hour to give your life to Christ and accept Him as your Savior.

---

(1) Exodus 20:13, KJV. (2) Matthew 5–7. (3) Romans 6:23, KJV. (4) Ezekiel 18:4, NKJV. (5) Galatians 3:24. (6) Ephesians 2:8–9, NKJV. (7) Cf. Galatians 3:1. (8) Exodus 20:7, KJV. (9) Proverbs 15:3, NKJV. (10) Psalm 99:5, NKJV. (11) 1 John 4:8, KJV. (12) Deuteronomy 28:58, NKJV. (13) Matthew 6:9, KJV. (14) Deuteronomy 5:11, NKJV. (15) Psalm 66:13–14, NKJV. (16) 1 John 1:7, NKJV. (17) Romans 10:13, NKJV. (18) Proverbs 29:1, NKJV.

This message was taken from *The Ten Commandments*, by Billy Graham, ©1958 (copyright renewed 1986, revised 1995, 2000) Billy Graham Evangelistic Association.

STEPS TO PEACE WITH GOD

1. GOD'S PURPOSE: PEACE AND LIFE

God loves you and wants you to experience peace and life—abundant and eternal.

THE BIBLE SAYS ...

"We have peace with God through our Lord Jesus Christ." *Romans 5:1, NIV*

"For God so loved the world that He gave His only begotten Son, that whoever believes in Him should not perish but have everlasting life." *John 3:16, NKJV*

"I have come that they may have life, and that they may have it more abundantly." *John 10:10, NKJV*

Since God planned for us to have peace and the abundant life right now, why are most people not having this experience?

2. OUR PROBLEM: SEPARATION

God created us in His own image to have an abundant life. He did not make us as robots to automatically love and obey Him, but gave us a will and a freedom of choice.

We chose to disobey God and go our own willful way. We still make this choice today. This results in separation from God.

THE BIBLE SAYS ...

"For all have sinned and fall short of the glory of God." *Romans 3:23, NIV*

"For the wages of sin is death, but the gift of God is eternal life in Christ Jesus our Lord." *Romans 6:23, NIV*

Our choice results in separation from God.

OUR ATTEMPTS

Through the ages, individuals have tried in many ways to bridge this gap ... without success ...

THE BIBLE SAYS ...

"There is a way that seems right to a man, but in the end it leads to death." *Proverbs 14:12, NIV*

"But your iniquities have separated you from your God; and your sins have hidden His face from you, so that He will not hear."
Isaiah 59:2, NKJV

There is only one remedy for this problem of separation.

3. GOD'S REMEDY: THE CROSS

Jesus Christ is the only answer to this problem. He died on the cross and rose from the grave, paying the penalty for our sin and bridging the gap between God and people.

THE BIBLE SAYS ...

"For there is one God and one mediator between God and men, the man Christ Jesus." *1 Timothy 2:5, NIV*

"For Christ also suffered once for sins, the just for the unjust, that He might bring us to God." *1 Peter 3:18, NKJV*

"But God demonstrates his own love for us in this: While we were still sinners, Christ died for us." *Romans 5:8, NIV*

God has provided the only way ... we must make the choice ...

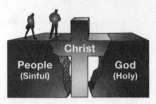

4. OUR RESPONSE: RECEIVE CHRIST

We must trust Jesus Christ and receive Him by personal invitation.

THE BIBLE SAYS ...

"Behold, I stand at the door and knock. If anyone hears My voice and opens the door, I will come in to him and dine with him, and he with Me."
Revelation 3:20, NKJV

"But as many as received Him, to them He gave the right to become children of God, to those who believe in His name."
John 1:12, NKJV

"If you confess with your mouth the Lord Jesus and believe in your heart that God has raised Him from the dead, you will be saved." *Romans 10:9, NKJV*

Are you here ... or here?

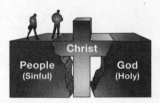

Is there any good reason why you cannot receive Jesus Christ right now?

How to receive Christ:

1. Admit your need. "I am a sinner."

2. Be willing to turn from your sins (repent).

3. Believe that Jesus Christ died for you on the cross and rose from the grave.

4. Through prayer, invite Jesus Christ to come in and control your life through the Holy Spirit. (Receive Him as your Lord and Savior.)

What to Pray:

Dear Lord Jesus,

I know that I am a sinner and need Your forgiveness. I believe that You died for my sins. I want to turn from my sins. I now invite You to come into my heart and life. I want to trust and follow You as Lord and Savior.

In Your Name. Amen.

Date	Signature

If you are committing your life to Christ, please let us know!
Billy Graham Evangelistic Association
1 Billy Graham Parkway, Charlotte, NC 28201-0001
1-877-2GRAHAM (1-877-247-2426)
billygraham.org

Decision magazine is published 11 times a year by the Billy Graham Evangelistic Association. Subscriptions are U.S. $12 per year (within North America). Please contact us for current rates or for subscription rates outside North America.

To order, send name and address, along with your payment, to *Decision* magazine, P.O. Box 668886, Charlotte, NC 28266-8886.

You can order using a credit card by calling toll-free 1-877-2GRAHAM (1-877-247-2426) in the United States (1-888-393-0003 in Canada) or by visiting our Web site at **decisionmag.org**.

New subscriptions may take 6–8 weeks to process and deliver in the United States and Canada (longer outside North America).